A SPECTRUM BOOK Prentice-Hall, Inc., Englewood Cliffs, New Jersey 07632

JEAN-PIERRE COHEN, M.D.
ROGER GOIRAND, M.D.

Pregnancy, Delivery, and Infant Care

YOUR BABY

Library of Congress Cataloging in Publication Data

Cohen, Jean Pierre.
   Your baby.

   (A Spectrum Book)
   Translation of Mon bébé.
   Includes indexes.
      1. Pregnancy.   2. Childbirth.   3. Infants (Newborn)
—Care and hygiene. ' I. Goirand, Roger, joint author.
II. Title.   [DNLM: 1. Pregnancy—Popular works.
2. Labor—Popular works.   3. Infant care—Popular works.
WQ 150 C677y]
RG525.C6613   649'.1   80-27884
ISBN 0-13-978130-7
ISBN 0-13-978122-6 (pbk.)

Original French language edition by Fernand Nathan Editeur,
Paris, France. Copyright by Fernand Nathan Editeur

10   9   8   7   6   5   4   3   2   1

Editorial/production supervision by Heath Lynn Silberfeld and Kimberly Mazur
Cover design by Honi Werner
Maufacturing buyer: Barbara A. Frick

ISBN 0-13-978130-7

ISBN 0-13-978122-6 {PBK.}

Prentice-Hall International, Inc., *London*
Prentice-Hall of Australia Pty. Limited, *Sydney*
Prentice-Hall Canada Inc., *Toronto*
Prentice-Hall of India Private Limited, *New Delhi*
Prentice-Hall of Japan, Inc., *Tokyo*
Prentice-Hall of Southeast Asia Pte. Ltd., *Singapore*
Whitehall Books Limited, *Wellington, New Zealand*

Jean-Pierre Cohen, M.D., is a pediatrician, and **Roger Goirand**, M.D., is a specialist in obstetrics and gynecology. Dr. Cohen teaches infant care and psychology at the Belle-de-Mai School of Midwifery at the Hospital Center of the University of Marseille, where Dr. Goirand has been director since 1966.

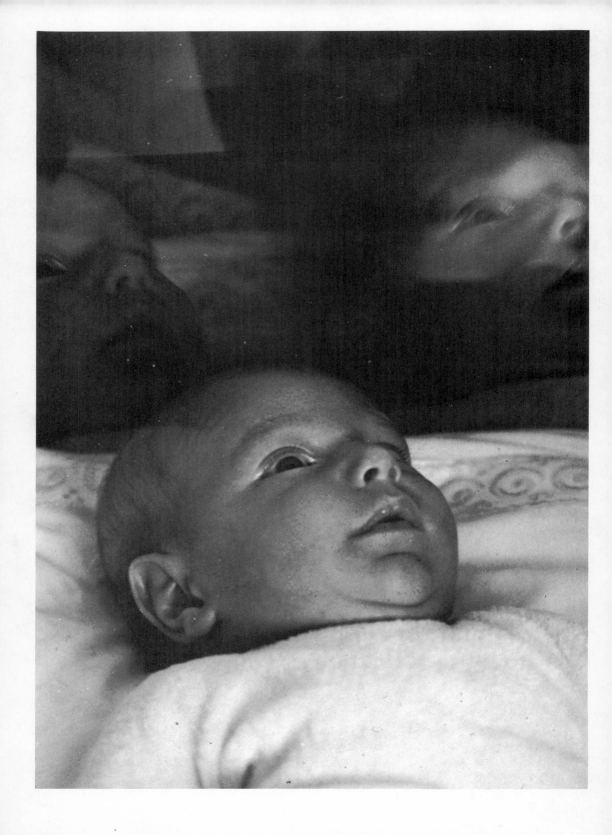

Contents

At a time when one sees many childcare books, we would like to present to you a book with a different focus. The events leading up to the birth of a child and the days immediately following are the subject of this book.

Until now, our profession has approached pregnancy and childbirth as separate subjects. In reality, everything that concerns the child to be born should be considered as one discipline. This discipline is called perinatal care, the Greek prefix *peri* meaning encircling. Thus, this term refers to all subjects concerning pregnancy, childbirth, and the days immediately following childbirth.

The three stages are intimately intertwined. A healthy pregnancy influences tremendously the delivery and health of the newborn infant. Today we assume that everyone is aware of this. In the past, however, family traditions and experiences were often the only resources available to the expectant mother. Now, to make sure that everything goes well, you have your doctor to assist you. The role of the doctor is extremely important, and our book is not designed to usurp this role. On the contrary, by making perinatal information available to you, we want to give you the means to assist your doctor with the job at hand. The more you know about your pregnancy and delivery, the more meaningful the birth of your child will be.

A veritable evolution has taken place in the past few years. The fatalities of the past have diminished. The role of the mother has changed, also. She can choose to become pregnant, and she actively participates in the delivery, often without heavy sedation. Some mothers receive no sedation and remain fully conscious for the duration of labor.

To be an active partner in childbirth, access to information becomes critical. The press, radio, and television present information, but often in an erratic manner. In this book, we give you the

Preface

essential information in a concise, accessible format. The facts are close at hand, freeing you from fears and hearsay. In addition, the facts about pregnancy and childbirth, information on heredity, prevention of illness in newborns, and infant care are also included. We examine each step of the way and anticipate as many of your questions as we can. We have avoided speculating about subjects that don't have definite answers or that do not pertain to a majority of women.

In conclusion, we hope that this book will take some of the mystery out of your pregnancy and, by making you more aware of what is going on, add to your joy.

P.S. Before publication of this book, several friends expressed amazement that both authors of this book were men. This reaction surprised us. During this time of new ideas about the roles of men and women, fathers have become more actively involved in the rearing of their children. As doctors, we are convinced that the birth of a child concerns both parents equally and that fathers will profit from reading these pages too.

ACKNOWLEDGMENTS

We would like to salute the competence and devotion of the midwives, nurses, and pediatric nurses who have worked with us. We owe them a debt of gratitude. We also would like to commend the secretaries who typed this manuscript for their patience.

1

To understand the various stages of the development of an egg, from fertilization to delivery, it is necessary to know the functions and placement of the organs in which the adventure of life begins. These organs are called the reproductive organs. For a long time, cultural taboos prevented the circulation of accurate information. Embarrassment prevented people from discussing reproduction. The demystification of sexuality and the processes that begin life allow us to examine these functions more clearly.

The reproductive organs include both hidden internal organs and visible external organs.

REPRODUCTIVE ORGANS

Internal

Internal organs consist of the uterus, the ovaries, the Fallopian tubes, and the vagina. They are located between the bladder and the rectum.

The uterus is a pear-shaped, muscular chamber. The upper section, the body of the organ, is larger and flatter than the lower section. The lower section, the neck of the uterus, is narrower and rounder. It is about 3 inches long, about 2 inches wide, and 1½ inches thick. If we examine the inside of the uterus, we would find a cavity covered by a thin mucous membrane. The cervix, situated at the base of the uterus, connects the uterine cavity to the vagina.

Baby's First Cradle: Your Body

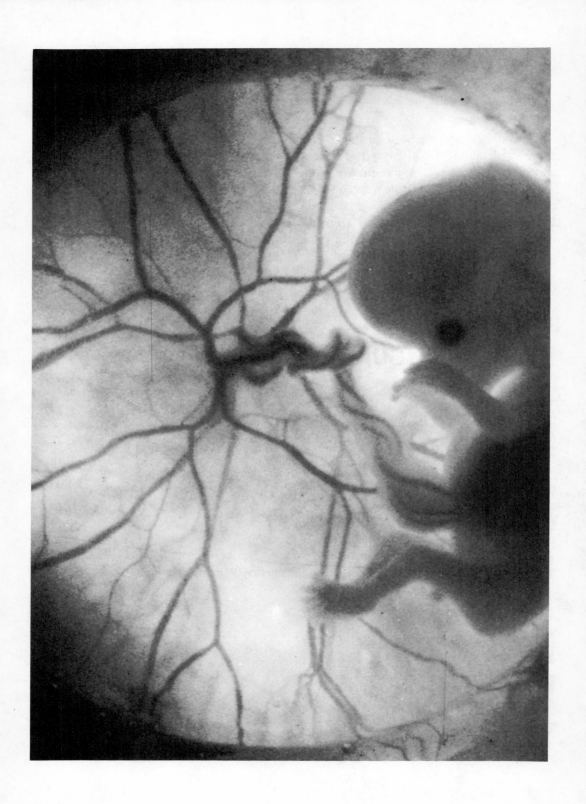

The ovaries, which rest on the wall of the pelvis, are almond-shaped. They are about 1 inch by ¾ inch, and about ³/₁₆ inch thick. Their irregular surfaces are covered with ridges. These ridges form the follicles that mature and release eggs. (This is explained in greater detail later.) The ovaries produce the eggs and secrete female hormones.

The Fallopian tubes are two tubes, each about 6 inches long, between the uterus and the ovaries. They are very thin and close to the uterus. Near the ovary they become larger in diameter and more bell-shaped. Fertilization of the egg takes place in the Fallopian tubes.

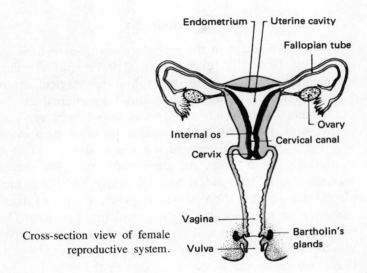

Cross-section view of female reproductive system.

The vagina is a canal 2 to 4 inches long. It connects the base of the uterus with the outside of the body. The vagina is very elastic and dilates easily during labor. The front wall is shorter than the back wall; a sort of "cul-de-sac" at the top of the vagina accounts for the difference in length.

External

The vulva consists of large, external lips and smaller, internal lips. The clitoris is positioned at the front of the internal lips. The urethra lies between the clitoris and the vagina.

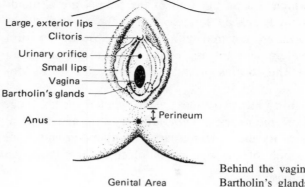

Large, exterior lips
Clitoris
Urinary orifice
Small lips
Vagina
Bartholin's glands

Anus
↕ Perineum

Genital Area

Behind the vagina, and on either side, Bartholin's glands lubricate the vagina.

The Gynecological Examination

An examination of the reproductive organs can be done in several ways. Generally, examinations fall into these groups: clinical examination, X-rays, ultrasonography, and surgical explorations.

The clinical examination includes an internal and an external examination. For an internal, one or two fingers are placed in the vagina while the other hand is used to press on the abdomen. In this way the doctor can determine the size and position of the uterus, ovaries, Fallopian tubes, and the peritoneum. (The peritoneum is a membrane that lines the abdominal cavity and holds the organs in place.) This examination is usually painless. To facilitate the examination, one must assume the gynecological position. Your doctor will advise you on this. The neck of the uterus may be examined visually by using a speculum attached to an eyepiece. (A speculum is an instrument that dilates a passage of the body for examination.)

An X-ray shows the entire uterine cavity, after injection of a contrast product. From an X-ray a doctor can see many things, including whether the Fallopian tubes are open. (This technique is used mainly for fertility tests.)

Ultrasonography is a process by which inaudible, high-frequency sound waves are bounced off internal parts of the body, or a developing fetus, and then are translated by electrical equipment into images of the organs or fetus being examined. As the density of the tissue being struck with sound waves changes, the image being projected changes. Doctors trained in the use of ultrasonography can interpret such images to help determine pregnancy, identify more than one fetus, and measure the diameter of the fetus's head to

Vaginal examination. Uterus is lifted by finger in the vagina; the other hand presses on the abdomen.

Normal uterus; tubes are open

Malformed uterus, here doubled

Tubes that are closed; fertility impossible

estimate how far advanced a pregnancy is. Ultrasound can also be used to identify various problems in fetal development, to locate the placenta, and to determine certain abnormalities that can develop. It can help to identify uterine tumors and to detect foreign bodies, such as an intrauterine device, that might be situated in the area being examined.

Laparoscopy is a surgical procedure that enables a doctor to see inside the abdominal cavity. It makes use of a laparoscope, an instrument that includes a tube and an optical device that lights the area being examined. The laparoscpe is inserted into the abdominal cavity through a small incision. Laparoscopy can sometimes determine whether a tubal pregnancy has occurred.

In amniocentesis, a needle is introduced into the abdominal cavity in such a way as to enter the amniotic sac without touching the fetus. Through this needle, up to 30 milliliters of amniotic fluid can be removed. A number of laboratory procedures may then be performed on the fluid to determine whether the fetus is being affected by certain health factors. The procedure can also tell the sex of the fetus. Amniocentesis may not be done any earlier than 15 to 18 weeks after conception. It is performed under local anesthesia. Although it can alert the physician to the existence of certain problems, like all surgical procedures, it does entail some risk—to both the mother and fetus.

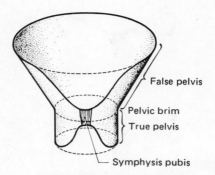

└ False pelvis

└ Pelvic brim
└ True pelvis

└ Symphysis pubis   Simplified pelvic structure.

The Pelvis

The pelvis is a bowl-shaped group of bones at the base of the trunk. The hip bones form the sides of the pelvis. The shape is completed in the front by the symphysis pubis. In the back the hip bones are separated by the sacral triangle, which is at the base of the backbone. Together, these bones form the pelvic girdle.

The pelvic structures form a sort of funnel. The bowl shape narrows into a columnlike form, with the notch-shaped symphysis pubis in the front. The larger, bowl-shaped section is referred to as the false pelvis, and the neck section is referred to as the true pelvis. The two are joined at the pelvic brim.

The true pelvis has a tremendous importance in obstetrics, because the child must pass through this area during childbirth. (The child passes the pelvic brim, and leaves through the true pelvic area.)

The pelvic brim separates the false pelvis from the true pelvis.

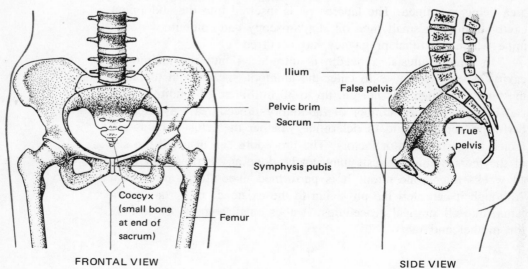

Ilium

Pelvic brim
Sacrum

False pelvis

True pelvis

Symphysis pubis

Coccyx
(small bone
at end of
sacrum)

Femur

FRONTAL VIEW   SIDE VIEW

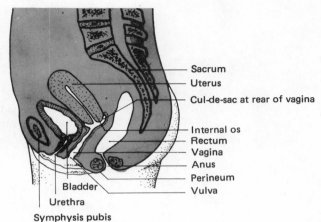

Sacrum
Uterus
Cul-de-sac at rear of vagina

Internal os
Rectum
Vagina
Anus
Perineum
Vulva

Bladder
Urethra
Symphysis pubis

Side view of bones and organs.

Base of true pelvis.

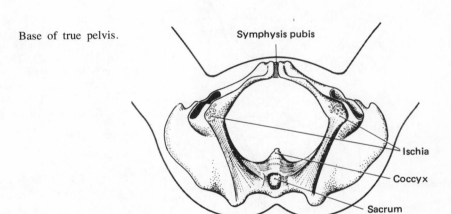

Symphysis pubis

Ischia

Coccyx

Sacrum

By picturing a person lying in the gynecological position, it is easier to visualize the placement of these anatomical parts. On top is the symphysis pubis, the frontal joining of the base of the hipbones. Next are the ischia, which are the parts of the hipbones we sit on. Further down, we find the sacral triangle and the coccyx bones. Attached to these bony structures are a series of muscles and tissue called the pelvic floor.

The Pelvic Floor The pelvic floor is composed of muscles at the base of the pelvic bones. These muscles lift the anus and form the external anal area. During childbirth these muscles play an important role.

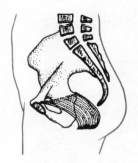

Pelvic floor. The muscle that lifts the anus originates across the mid-pelvis and then goes behind and down to the anus.

PELVIC FLOOR

Cleft in sphincter muscle

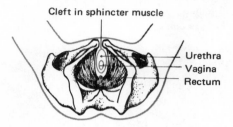

Urethra
Vagina
Rectum

Bottom view of muscles that surround the genitals. The vagina rests in a break in the muscle pair.

Cross-section view of the pelvis.

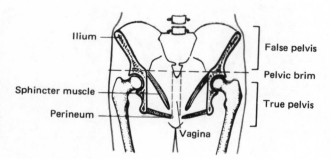

Ilium

False pelvis

Pelvic brim

Sphincter muscle

True pelvis

Perineum

Vagina

The Perineum

The perineum closes the rear section of the pelvic floor and acts as the dividing line between the vulva and the anus. Between the two, muscles from the base of the hipbone and from the sphincter muscle of the anus meet at the perineum. The skin covering this section of the body is very thin. Normally, the distance between the vulva and the anus measures between 1½ and 2 inches.

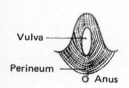

Vulva

Perineum

Anus

These tissues are very elastic at all times. During pregnancy, they become even more elastic than usual to facilitate childbirth. Water retention causes the tissues to retain elasticity.

THE MENSTRUAL CYCLE

Approximately every 28 days a flow of blood leaves the uterus through the vagina. The flow lasts between three and seven days and is referred to as a monthly period. Periods appear during puberty (between 10 and 16 years of age) and continue until menopause (between 40 and 55 years of age). The reproductive life of a woman is divided by these menstrual cycles, which do not usually occur during pregnancy and nursing.

Menstrual blood does not clot and is mixed with water. The flow comes from the lining of the uterus. This lining changes significantly during the course of the menstrual cycle. After a period, the lining is very thin ($^1/_{32}$ of an inch). Because of hormones secreted by the ovaries, the lining increases in thickness to $^3/_{16}$ of an inch. If there is no pregnancy at this point, the superficial part of the lining flows out of the body, and a new cycle begins.

The Ovaries

Every month an egg is released from the ovary. Ovulation takes place approximately 15 days before the onset of the next period. The egg cell has a particular character that distinguishes it from the other body cells. Normally, cells that make up blood and body tissues contain 46 chromosomes. Reproductive cells contain 23 chromosomes.

Egg with cells that encircle it

Growth of follicle

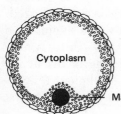

Cytoplasm

Mature egg nucleus   Development of Graafian follicle.

Of the 400,000 to 500,000 egg cells in the ovaries from birth, only 400, at the most, will be dropped into the pelvis. Each egg that is dropped is surrounded by a layer of cells and a group of small, undeveloped eggs. Each egg and layer of cells is called a follicle.

At each cycle several of these follicles begin to develop, but only one will mature and drop into the pelvis. The mature follicle is called the Graafian follicle. The Graafian follicle gets larger as it approaches the entrance of the ovary. At this point it is about .0015 to .0055 of an inch wide. The follicle bursts forth from the ovary into the Fallopian tube. It ruptures, releasing the small, undeveloped eggs and the large, mature egg. This moment is referred to as ovulation. A few moments before ovulation, the mouth of the Fallopian tube moves toward the ovary. The follicle is almost snatched from the ovary by the Fallopian tube before it bursts. The empty follicle shell crumples up and forms corpus luteum, which secretes the hormones estrogen and progesterone.

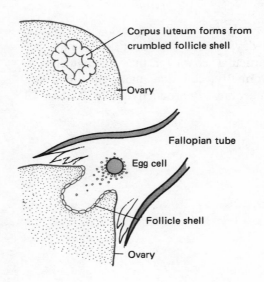

Estrogen is secreted continually, and progesterone is secreted after ovulation. Progesterone disappears if the egg is not fertilized. Estrogens stimulate the development of the uterus, the vagina, the breasts, and the other secondary sex characteristics. Progesterone regulates reproductive functions. It prepares the lining of the uterus to receive a fertilized egg and attaches the egg to the lining. Progesterone affects the lining of the uterus in two stages. During the first

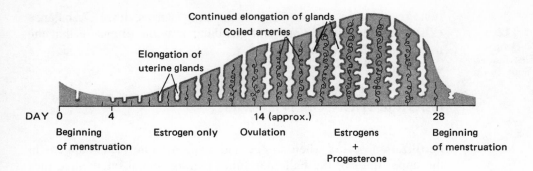

Continued elongation of glands

Coiled arteries

Elongation of
uterine glands

DAY 0	4		14 (approx.)		28
Beginning of menstruation		Estrogen only	Ovulation	Estrogens + Progesterone	Beginning of menstruation

stage the lining develops and is maintained. During the second stage glands are stimulated to form mucus and glycogen, which is a starch. Progesterone also causes the lining to develop in a ridgelike pattern. If no pregnancy occurs, progesterone production drops, and menstruation occurs. If pregnancy occurs, the ovaries continue to secrete progesterone, and menstruation does not occur. Progesterone may be responsible for some mood changes in women.

Hormonal changes also affect body temperature in women. During ovulation, basal temperature rises about .4 to .8°F above normal for the individual. After the menstrual period, it drops back down. If a pregnancy begins, body temperature stays slightly elevated until the end of the fourth month. Through daily temperature readings, it may be possible to chart hormonal changes. Examination of vaginal mucus also helps to determine these changes.

Regulation of the Menstrual Cycle

The hypothalamus and the central nervous system control ovulation. The anterior lobe of the gland secretes hormones that stimulate the other glands of the body. Besides the ovaries, these glands include the thyroid gland and the adrenal glands. The chemical that stimulates the ovaries to produce a follicle is called FSH (follicle-stimulating hormone). Another hormone from the hypothalamus causes the corpus luteum to form from the Graafian follicle. This hormone is called LH (luteinizing hormone).

In summary, a signal to ovulate leaves the hypothalamus and travels to the anterior lobe of the pituitary gland. The anterior lobe releases FSH, and the ovary begins to prepare a follicle. LH is also released from the anterior lobe, and the follicle bursts at the entrance of the Fallopian tube (ovulation). The shell of the follicle (corpus luteum) produces progesterone. If conception does not occur, the corpus luteum disintegrates immediately prior to menstruation, resulting in a steep drop in the progesterone level. A balance exists between the nervous and glandular systems to ensure that the monthly cycles continue.

FERTILIZATION OF THE EGG

Fertilization occurs when an egg and a sperm unite. This happens in the upper third of the Fallopian tube. During sexual intercourse millions of sperm are released into the upper portion of the vagina. From there they travel to the uterus and up the Fallopian tubes. The travel of the sperm is aided by contractions in the uterus and tubes and secretions of body fluid. Of the millions that are released, only about 15 to 50 actually get to the upper section of the Fallopian tubes, and only one will fertilize the egg.

The egg is a large cell in comparison with the sperm. The egg contains nutritive substances and is surrounded by follicle cells. Sperm cells measure about $\frac{1}{500}$ of an inch (51 micrometers) long. They consist of a head (containing 23 chromosomes), a body, and a whiplike tail. This tail gives them mobility.

Sperm cells can reach that part of the Fallopian tube where fertilization takes place about 1 to 1½ hours after they are released into the vagina. Sperm travel at a speed that has been estimated at between 1.5 and 3 millimeters a minute. Estimates of how long sperm cells remain capable of fertilizing an ovum range from 1 to 4 days.

Sperm cells cluster around the egg. If one of them penetrates the membrane surrounding the egg, this membrane retracts, and no other sperm cells can penetrate the egg.

The follicles around the egg are then repelled by a substance secreted by the Fallopian tubes. The remaining sperm cells disperse.

On entering the egg, the sperm cell loses its tail, and the body of the sperm cell forms part of the aster that forms between the nuclei of the egg and the sperm. The aster splits and makes a spin-

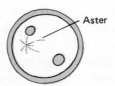 Aster

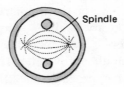 Spindle

dle. The chromosomes of each egg then group on either side of the fertilized egg. In this way the fertilized cell has 46 chromosomes. As cell division occurs, each new cell will have 46 chromosomes.

DEVELOPMENT OF THE CHILD, FROM FERTILIZATION TO BIRTH

After fertilization the egg, aided by contractions in the Fallopian tube, travels to the uterus. By the fourth day the fertilized egg has entered the uterine cavity. At about the sixth day it begins to attach itself to the lining of the uterus in a phenomenon called *nidation*.

During these first days the fertilized cell begins to divide. About 30 hours after fertilization there are 2 cells. By the fiftieth hour there are 4 cells. By the third day there are 16 cells. At this stage the egg resembles a small berry (morula stage). The global volume has not increased because the egg is still surrounded by the membrane.

Migration. Fertilized egg travels to the uterus.

This membrane disappears during the fourth day. The egg now contains 30 to 60 cells. These cells are grouped on one side of the egg and are called the embryonic plate. The rest of the egg contains liquid. Around the edge of the egg are peripheral cells called the trophoblast. Eventually, the cells grouping on the wall of the egg will form the embryo, and the cells on the edges of the egg will form the placenta and surrounding membranes.

Nesting of the Egg in the Uterine Wall (Nidation)

Between about the fifth and the tenth days the egg attaches itself to the uterine wall. The endometrium (mucosal lining) has been prepared by the hormone progesterone. The mucus is about ⅜ of an inch thick. The part of the egg containing fertilized cells nests in the mucus.

Once the contact between the embryonic cells and the endometrium (or uterine lining) has been made, a sort of giant cell with several large nuclei begins to grow within the uterine mucous membrane. This cell is called the syntrophoblast. It contains enzymes that cause the uterine lining to open up paths to push nutritive elements to the egg. By the tenth day the egg has attached itself completely to the uterus.

During these four days the embryonic cells have changed. Two groups of cells have evolved, external cells, called the ectoderm (or ectoblast), and internal cells, called the endoderm. During the eighth day the ectoderm cells begin to form a circle within the egg. This circular cavity is called the amnion. At the same time the endoderm also forms a cavity. This cavity is called the umbilical vesicle. By the tenth day the wall of the egg has made contact with paths supplying nutrients from the uterus. The systems of the child and mother are joined through these channels. Circulation occurs through these channels also.

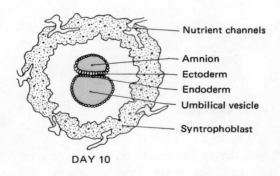

Nutrient channels
Amnion
Ectoderm
Endoderm
Umbilical vesicle
Syntrophoblast

DAY 10

The Embryonic Stage:
The Formation of Organs

At this point the embryo resembles a disk. Toward the end of the second week a furrow appears on the bottom side of the disk. The furrow ends in a small bulge, called Hensen's node. A third group of cells, called the mesoderm, grows from this furrow. This third group of cells forms between the ectoderm and the endoderm. The ectoderm and the endoderm are still in contact with each other. Later, they separate, when the pharyngeal membrane forms. At one end of the pharyngeal membrane the throat of the infant will form; at the other end the anus and the exterior genital organs will form from the cloacal membrane.

At this stage the embryo has three layers of cells. All the child's organs grow from these three groups of cells. The ectoderm

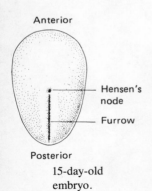

Anterior

Hensen's
node

Furrow

Posterior
15-day-old
embryo.

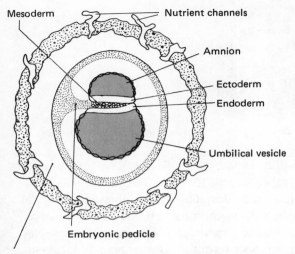

Mesoderm — Nutrient channels

Amnion

Ectoderm

Endoderm

Umbilical vesicle

Embryonic pedicle

Cross-section of 15-day-old embryo. From the 12th day, a cavity forms between the trophoblast and the embryonic knob, leaving the embryonic pedicle, which supplies sustenance and will become the umbilical cord.

will become the central nervous system, forming the nerves, the skin, the hair, and the nerves of the eyes and ears. The endoderm forms the esophagus, the liver, the lungs, and the other internal organs. The mesoderm forms the bones, the muscles, the backbone, the sex glands, the heart, and the blood.

By the seventeenth day the embryo is pear-shaped and measures about 1 millimeter. The spinal cord is formed, and the spinal column begins to grow. The spinal cord itself starts the growth of the spinal column. The column closes by itself; then the secondary stage of growth takes place.

This chain reaction marks the growth of all the developing parts. Before a new stage of development takes place, proteins are formed. When it is time for the new cells to grow, the chromosomes and genes are activated by enzymes. The proteins are used in the creation of the new cells. When one stage is finished, proteins for the next stage arrive; genes and chromosomes are stimulated by the enzymes, and the next stage of growth takes places. This process is called induction.

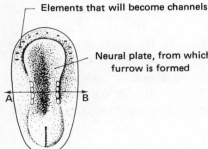

Elements that will become channels

Neural plate, from which the neural furrow is formed

A B

This view of the embryo shows the neural furrow, which closes between the 22nd and 27th days and becomes the neural tube.

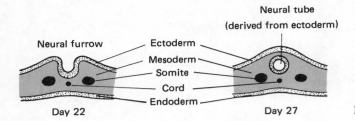

Neural tube
(derived from ectoderm)

Neural furrow — Ectoderm

— Mesoderm

— Somite

— Cord

— Endoderm

Day 22

Day 27

Development of the neural tube.

From the twenty-fifth to the thirty-fourth days the anterior section of the neural tube begins to form. At first, only three cervical (neck) vertebrae start to develop. By the thirty-fifth day, all five of the neck vertebrae will be forming. The development of the nervous system is already quite extensive. Elements of the muscles, backbone, and cartilage are also forming. The embryo is increasing in volume and has lost its disklike appearance. The developing umbilical cord is attached to the front. The intestines are forming outside the main part of the embryo. They are not fully joined to the rest of the embryo until the beginning of the third month.

At this point the back of the embryo seems abnormally large. The nervous system is developing very rapidly. The cells divide every eight hours. At the end of 24 hours the volume of the embryo has increased geometrically by eight.

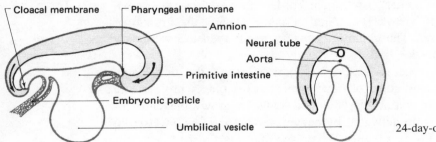

Cloacal membrane — Pharyngeal membrane

— Amnion

Neural tube

Aorta

— Primitive intestine

— Embryonic pedicle

Umbilical vesicle —

24-day-old embryo.

By the third week formative elements of the veins and arteries are also growing. They form little channels, which start to grow toward the ventral (frontal) side of the embryo. Between the nineteenth and twenty-second days, they join and form the cardiac tube. Soon this will develop into the heart. By the twenty-seventh day the embryo measures about ⅛ of an inch. By the thirty-seventh day it measures about ½ of an inch. The heart is formed by the end of the tenth week. At this point the embryo is about 1½ inches long.

At three weeks it would be difficult to distinguish a human embryo from that of any other mammal. The head looks quite large.

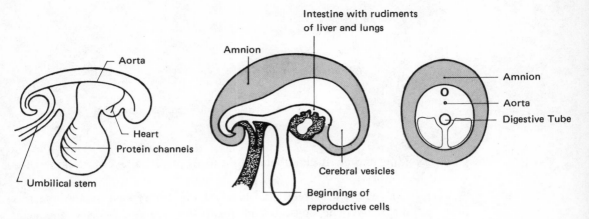

Aorta

Heart

Protein channels

Umbilical stem

Amnion

Intestine with rudiments
of liver and lungs

Cerebral vesicles

Beginnings of
reproductive cells

Amnion

Aorta

Digestive Tube

End of first month.

Although there are no eyes or ears, the places where they will eventually grow are visible. On about the twenty-sixth day the upper extremities make their appearance, and on about the twenty-eighth day the lower extremities begin to form. The esophagus begins to grow, and the heart begins to beat by the end of the first month. The major internal organs have all begun to develop.

During the second month external characteristics will take shape. It becomes more obvious that the embryo is a human embryo. The head enlarges; the chest region becomes fuller because the pericardium (a protective membrane around the heart) develops; the liver enlarges. The face of the embryo rests on the growing pericardium. Below the pericardium the umbilical cord is attached to the body.

Some muscles form on the head, the trunk, and the extremities. The hemispheres of the brain are side by side. The cardiac tube has a distinct form now. A bulb has begun to form, and tissues

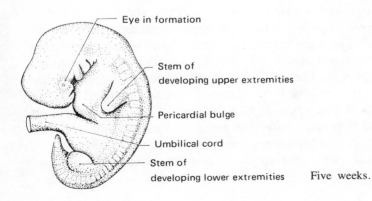

Eye in formation

Stem of
developing upper extremities

Pericardial bulge

Umbilical cord

Stem of
developing lower extremities

Five weeks.

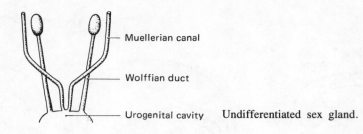

Muellerian canal

Wolffian duct

Urogenital cavity   Undifferentiated sex gland.

dividing the heart chambers begin to form. Two layers of skin cover the embryo.

By the sixth week, the head of the embryo dominates the rest of the body. The embryo appears to tilt forward, because the neck is bent at an angle. The bones of the jaw join and form the chin. The tongue also begins to grow at this time. The mouth and gums begin to form, and the external ear starts its development. Small buds appear at the ends of the extremities; later these become hands and feet. Furrows mark the places of future elbows and knees, and several days later, curves develop, marking those joints. The heart has attained its general form, and ribs start to form.

The sex glands appear, but they are neither male nor female at this point. Indeed, they have qualities of both sexes. Let us return to the twenty-first day. At that time cells leave the bladder, go through the intestine, and deposit themselves in the urogenital area of the embryo. They collect in an area called the Wolffian body. There they multiply and form the primitive sex glands. At this point, there are the Muellerian ducts and the Wolffian ducts. These two ducts connect to the urogenital cavity.

By the seventh week the embryo is about ¾ of an inch long. The back has straightened, the fingers can be differentiated from one another, and the palate has formed, but the tongue has not yet separated from it. The stomach has dilated and taken its position in the abdomen. Baby teeth have started to form, and muscle development progresses rapidly. The eyelids appear, and the spleen has also been formed. The brain continues to grow, and the intestine starts to function. The lungs make their first appearance during this time.

The cloaca is situated below the umbilical cord. The intestine, the urinary tract, and the genital tubes end in this cavity. During the seventh week a thin layer of tissue separates the urogenital tube and the intestinal tube. Later this thin tissue will become the perineum, and the anal canal will connect with the intestine. During the ninth week, the anus will open up to the exterior of the body.

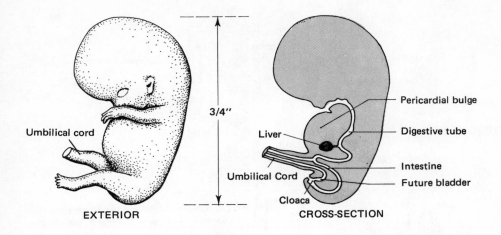

	Pericardial bulge
Liver	Digestive tube
	Intestine
Umbilical Cord	Future bladder
Cloaca	

Umbilical cord

3/4"

EXTERIOR   CROSS-SECTION

By the eighth week the embryo measures a little over 1 inch. The nose has flattened, and the eyes have opened. The fingers have assumed their characteristic structure, and the abdomen is rounder. The head becomes more erect. The liver continues to develop, and the diaphragm makes its appearance. The embryo begins to make small, imprecise movements. One can see an outline of the breasts. The external ear is recognizable, and the testicles or ovaries start to form. If the embryo is female, the two Muellerian ducts fuse their lower sections to form the uterine-vaginal duct. Later this will become the uterus and the upper section of the vagina.

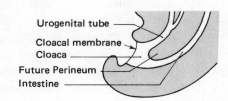

Urogenital tube
Cloacal membrane
Cloaca
Future Perineum
Intestine

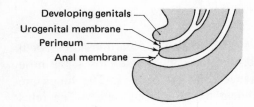

Developing genitals
Urogenital membrane
Perineum
Anal membrane

The perineal tissue makes contact with the cloacal membrane, dividing the urogenital cavity and the anal cavity.

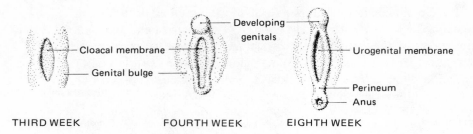

THIRD WEEK   FOURTH WEEK   EIGHTH WEEK

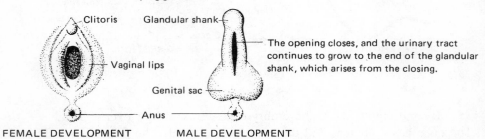

FEMALE DEVELOPMENT   MALE DEVELOPMENT

ELEVENTH WEEK

Sexual differentiation.

By the tenth week the embryo measures 1½ inches. The head now aligns with the axis of the body; the lips appear; the extremities are well formed; and fingernails begin to grow. Vocal cords begin to form; bones solidify; kidneys start to function; the muscles of the anal region grow; the eyelids join one another over the eyeball.

Organs characteristic of the opposite sex atrophy. In male embryos testicles begin to secrete androgens. This causes the Muellerian ducts to regress. In the future only male anatomy will develop. In female embryos Muellerian ducts continue to develop. Later these will become the Fallopian tubes, the uterus, and the upper portion of the vagina. By the end of the tenth week these organs are almost in place. The growth of the embryo accelerates, and we will refer to it as the fetus from now until the time of birth. Let us examine the fetal stage.

Development of the Organs in the Fetal Stage

At the beginning of the twelfth week the fetus measures about 2¼ inches. The cheeks form on the face; the palate closes; the nose assumes its customary appearance; bile is secreted. The lungs are making progress, and development of the eye continues. The fetus now has three layers of skin.

By the sixteenth week the face of the fetus takes on a human appearance. The eyes, nose, and ears are clearly marked, and hair begins to grow. Secretions accumulate in the intestine, and many bones are clearly identifiable. Joints appear, hair pushes its way through the skin, and the sebaceous glands develop. The skin is reddish in color, very fine in texture, and transparent. Spontaneous muscular activity begins; the fetus flexes its fist, and the mother is aware of movement.

By the fifth month the fetus is almost 1 foot long and weighs about 1 pound. The bones of the nose have hardened. A soft, downy substance has covered the skin to protect it. Movement of the arms and legs is more sharply defined, and the child can scratch. A cycle of sleeping and waking has begun, and the fetus reacts to loud noises. The sucking instinct has asserted itself, and hair is clearly visible. Eyebrows also appear. Of great importance is the continuing maturation of the spinal cord.

During the sixth month the body is thin, but well proportioned. Teeth can be seen in the gums, and the nostrils have opened. Characteristic lines of development can be traced on the skull. The first reflexes appear, and often the child will kick and move its hands. The fetus sleeps often. The child begins to develop its individual character. The fetus has grown another inch and weighs about 2¼ pounds.

 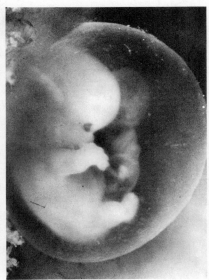

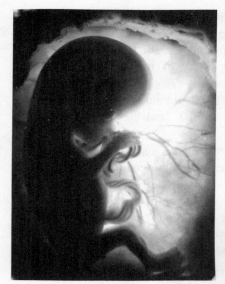

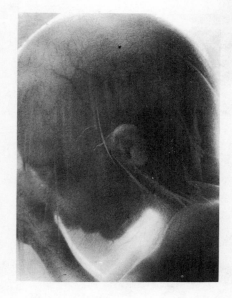

By the seventh month, the skin of the fetus is wrinkled and red. Development of the vital organs is nearly complete, and the fetus now needs to accumulate some extra weight. The respiratory system has not yet matured. If the fetus were to be born at this time, great care would have to be exercised. The baby would be very lively, however, if born during the seventh month. The newborn would open its eyes and be able to look around and suck on its thumb.

Cellular development of the brain is a hotly debated subject in the prenatal field. However, certain facts are widely accepted. By the third month significant cellular growth begins. This stage of growth is finished during the sixth month, with six layers of cells. After this stage of brain development the nervous system develops more fully. By the seventh month the nerves grow, lengthen, and assume their characteristic forms and functions. The fetus will eventually be born with 10 to 14 billion nerves, each one able to react with 10,000 nearby nerves. To understand the development of the nervous system better, imagine the beginnings of the telephone system. It all started with Dr. Bell uttering a few words into a primitive phone. Soon small, urban telephone systems sprang up. From these urban networks, national and international communication systems developed. Fetal brain development can be compared to the growth of this system.

Indeed, the central nervous system develops along a continuum from simplicity to great complexity, from purely reflex function to a capability for such involved phenomena as seeing and hearing. The sense of hearing is very important to the fetus. Although it exists in an insulated world, it can hear the mother's heartbeat, voice, and sounds of her digestive organs. The fetus also reacts to loud sounds outside the mother's body.

By the eighth month the fetus is about 18 inches long and weighs between 5 and 6 pounds. A layer of fat begins to form under the skin; wrinkles become less pronounced, and the body takes on a rounder, more babylike, appearance. In males the testicles descend from the scrotum at this time. Fingernails reach the ends of the fingertips. The baby's head turns toward the base of the mother's pelvis, and the child moves frequently.

By the ninth month the fetus measures approximately 20 inches and weighs 6 or more pounds. The soft, protective covering on the skin is lost prior to birth. The brain matures to the point that is normal for newborns. The baby is now ready to be born.

The Placenta, the Surrounding Membranes, and Embryonic Fluids

We have already discussed how the trophoblast comes in contact with the maternal ducts on the uterine lining of the mother and how space is created in the egg for the fetus to grow.

After this development, the trophoblast grows quickly and forms a spiny membrane around the egg. This spiny coating is called the chorion. Beneath the spiny covering of the chorion other tissues are also growing. As the egg gets larger, the spiny coating is lost, and these tissues below the coating become the placenta.

The mucous lining of the uterus undergoes changes during pregnancy and is given a special name: the decidua. By 4½ months the fetus has become so large that the sac surrounding it makes contact with the walls of the mother's uterus. The sac and the wall of the uterus are then joined.

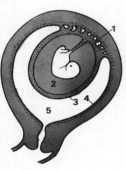

1. Placenta
2. Amniotic fluid
3. Egg sac
4. Uterine wall
5. Uterine cavity
6. Joining of the egg sac and the uterine wall

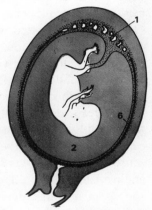

BEFORE 4½ MONTHS   AFTER 4½ MONTHS

At this point the fetus is surrounded by the amniotic fluid and attached to an umbilical cord. These are all enclosed by layers of membranes, consisting of an outer layer of tissue, the chorion, and an internal lining filled with amniotic fluid. As mentioned above, at 4½ months these linings are all joined to one another and to the wall of the uterus. The umbilical cord is about as wide as a finger at the time of birth. The cord contains two small arteries and a vein, which are surrounded by a gelatinous substance. The cord attaches to the mother and the fetus, and the two arteries transport nutritive

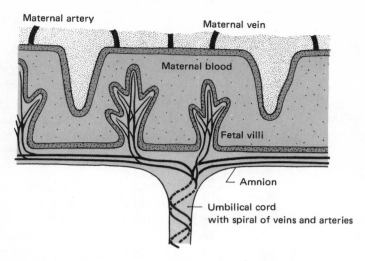

Maternal artery
Maternal vein
Maternal blood
Fetal villi
Amnion
Umbilical cord
with spiral of veins and arteries

substances to the fetus and wastes away from the fetus. A cross section of the wall of the placenta is shown.

The villi of the fetus are small tentacles imbedded in the mother's circulatory system. Oxygenated blood arrives from the mother in a small artery and returns by way of two veins. These two veins join other circulatory veins in the uterus. The fetal blood travels up the umbilical cord to the fetal villi, where it rids itself of wastes and takes oxygen and other necessary substances. The reoxygenated blood then returns to the fetus via the umbilical cord. It is interesting to note that the vein, not an artery, carries the oxygenated blood back to the fetus. Also, the blood of the fetus and that of the mother never mix. The two systems are separated by the thin cell walls of the fetal villi, through which all exchanges are made.

One element that can traverse the placental barrier, however, is the Rh antigen present in an Rh-positive fetus being carried by an Rh-negative mother. If such transfer does occur, and to the degree that it occurs, the antigen may cause the Rh-negative mother's body to create antibodies in opposition to the Rh antigen. If these antibodies cross the placental barrier back into the fetus's bloodstream, they can create serious, even fatal, problems for the fetus.

This phenomenon seems to be slow and variable, and its seriousness apparently increases with successive pregnancies. It can arise from the mating of an Rh-negative woman and an Rh-positive man. However, it does not always occur, and medical measures can often prevent serious damage if it does. Be sure to discuss the matter with your doctor and see if it applies to you.

The Role
of the Placenta

Essentially, the placenta is the means for all exchanges between the mother and the fetus. As already mentioned, it is through the placenta that the fetus receives oxygen, because the fetus, surrounded with amniotic fluid, cannot breathe. Nutrients, such as water, salts, calcium, vitamins, and sugars, pass through the placenta's filterlike system. The placenta manufactures proteins from elements of the mother's blood.

The placenta acts as a barrier against most important germs. However, certain germs can penetrate when the placenta is beginning to form during early pregnancy. The smallest viruses are also able to pass through at any time. Any of these viruses can hurt the developing fetus. One of the most notorious is rubella, or German measles. Medications, anesthetics antibodies from the mother, and substances that protect the newborn from attacking microbes also pass through the placenta to the fetus.

The placenta secretes a hormone called human chorionic gonadotropin, called HCG for short. HCG is a backup to the corpus luteum, ensuring that enough progesterone is produced. It shows up in the urine of a pregnant woman about a week after her first missed menstrual period, and is the hormone measured in pregnancy tests. Through modern testing (details of pregnancy tests are covered later) it can be determined in a few hours if a woman is pregnant. Also, hormonal tests can often indicate whether pregnancy is progressing normally.

The placenta also secretes estrogens that are normally secreted by the ovary.

Amniotic Fluid

Amniotic fluid is clear, and the uterus contains somewhat less than a quart at the end of a pregnancy. This fluid is secreted by the fetal membranes. The fetus also eliminates urine. The fetus absorbs small amounts of amniotic fluid daily, and wastes in the fluid are eliminated through the placenta. The fetus floats and moves in this liquid. It also protects the fetus from shocks and infections. At the onset of labor, this liquid is released from the body when the bag of waters breaks.

HEREDITY AND SEX

Long before genetic laws were known, some of the general principles were discovered through experience. To some extent, this primitive knowledge was used to control the results of reproduction.

Genetics was not studied in a systematic way until the end of the nineteenth century. By observing successive generations of garden peas for eight years, a monk named Gregor Mendel was able to establish the laws of heredity. The importance of Mendel's discoveries, however, was not recognized. In 1875 Oskar Hertwig, a German embryologist, observed the union of the sperm and egg of a sea urchin. Chromosomes were not discovered until 1890, and around 1900 researchers rediscovered Mendel's laws. It was then that Mendel was recognized as the father of genetics. The contribution of Thomas Hunt Morgan and his students to the study of genetics is considerable. Their work with fruit flies confirmed the studies of Mendel and proved that heredity is determined by chromosomes. Morgan won the Nobel Prize in Physiology and Medicine in 1933.

The Chromosomes

Some animals, such as amoebas, are made up of single cells. Others are made up of billions of cells, grouped by function.

Cells are composed of two parts, the nucleus and the cytoplasm. These two elements depend on each other in a very complex manner. Cells take nutrients supplied by the blood and turn them into products that the organism can use. This occurs mainly in the cytoplasm of each cell.

Geneticists are able to study the chromosomes and classify them by taking pictures of them as cells divide. The chromosomes are most visible just before the cell that is dividing splits into two cells. These photos are enlarged and studied carefully. Chromosomes can be grouped in pairs according to an international classification.

The number of chromosomes in each cell is the same in any given species. This number is normally an even number, because chromosomes are paired which is why we say 2 N chromosomes. Fruit flies have 4 pairs, cats have 19 pairs, pigs have 20 pairs, sheep have 27 pairs, cows have 30 pairs, horses have 33 pairs, and dogs have 39 pairs. Human beings have 23 pairs of chromosomes, 46 in all.

Single cell before division. The chromosomes are in the nucleus and are invisible.

In the beginning of the division, the chromosomes become visible.

The chromosomes replicate and line up between opposing poles.

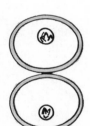

Two identical cells result from the division.

Determination of Sex

Of these 46 chromosomes, 44 are autosomes; that is, they are the same in both men and women. The two other chromosomes determine sex. In women, the sex chromosomes are identical and are called XX. In men the two chromosomes are different and are called XY.

Until fertilization, reproductive cells contain only N chromosomes, and not $2\,N$. Human reproductive cells contain 22 autosomes and one sex chromosome totaling 23 chromosomes. Female cells contain two XX, and male cells contain an XY. Female egg cells contain only one X, and male sperm cells contain either one X or one Y.

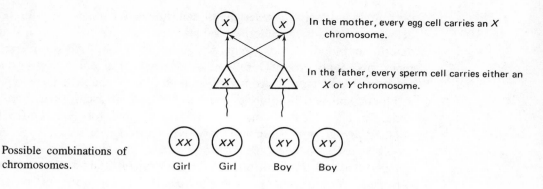

In the mother, every egg cell carries an *X* chromosome.

In the father, every sperm cell carries either an *X* or *Y* chromosome.

Possible combinations of chromosomes.

XX Girl XX Girl XY Boy XY Boy

The results of fertilization are as follows:

Egg X + sperm X = XX, resulting in a female.
Egg X + sperm Y = XY, resulting in a male.

One can see, therefore, that the sex of the child is fixed from the moment of conception and that the sperm cell determines the sex of the child.

Parents have long been preoccupied with the sex of their unborn children. Egyptian women urinated on barley and wheat to determine the outcome of their pregnancies. Since then, other imaginative methods have been used to determine the sex of unborn children. Among the factors considered have been time of conception, age of parents, eye examinations, and esoteric and occult practices.

The only conclusive way to determine the sex of a fetus at the present time is through amniocentesis, as discussed earlier in this chapter. This test, which can detect certain abnormalities in the developing fetus, is not performed solely to determine sex.

Laws of Heredity

From the many experiments on the fruit fly, geneticists can precisely locate the position of a specific trait on chromosomes. This position is called the locus. We know of 400 distinct traits in fruit flies, who have only four pairs of chromosomes. The longest chromosomes contain the greatest number of traits.

The chromosomes are in pairs, with each locus containing a gene. If the trait being examined has the same gene on both pairs of chromosomes, the person is homozygous for that trait. If two different genes are on the chromosome pair, with the dominant gene giving the trait, the person is heterozygous for the trait. For example, an individual's blood type is determined by genes. Red blood cells carry certain characteristic substances, called A, B, and O, that determine blood types: group A, group B, group AB (universal recipients), and group O (universal donors). If a child receives a gene for blood type A from both parents, he or she will have type A blood, and will be homozygous in this trait. If a child receives a gene for type A from one parent, and a gene for type O from another parent, the child will have type A blood, because type A blood genes dominate type O blood genes. However, this child is heterozygous in this trait and could pass on O blood to his or her offspring. These principles apply to all combinations of blood groups.

These facts become very important when determining the paternity of a child. Although it is not yet possible to determine conclusively that a man has fathered a child, it is possible to rule out paternity through blood tests.

In cases of inheriting a dominant trait, the subject can pass on one half of the inherited trait to offspring. Other characteristics are recessive. One example is albinoism, the lack of pigment in the body, resulting in white hair, pink pupils, and very light skin. Both parents may appear normal. Because both carry the recessive gene, however, the child may inherit the albino trait.

If a marriage takes place between close relatives, the risk of an undesirable trait rises dramatically, because common grandparents are shared. A good place to study this type of marriage is in the old European dynastic families. There was a great deal of intermarriage in order to produce political alliances. As a result, certain physical features became associated with these families. The Bourbons of France had a distinctive nose, and the Hapsburgs of Europe often had a protruding lower jaw.

Other inherited traits are more subtle and are more difficult to pinpoint from generation to generation. In an infant, one might see a characteristic eye shape, expression, or a smile that reminds one of a long-dead relative. A group of traits peculiar to the family can often be picked out easily. Other infants do not seem to inherit many family traits. The color of the hair does not belong to any close relatives. The eye color may be different from that of other family members. A blond child may be born into a family of brunettes. Parents who are short in stature may have a child who grows up to be tall.

Thus heredity determines many factors, both important and unimportant. It is impossible to determine the role of heredity alone on a person's development. Things such as intelligence, personality, and behavior are partly determined by millions of genes. Aside from the biochemical aspect of intelligence, one must admit that environment and education play a tremendous role. All of these factors add to the end result.

If a child with a lot of intelligence is raised in a healthy environment and receives a good education, the person's natural gifts will probably develop quite fully. If a person has average gifts, then the role of education and environment becomes more crucial to his or her intellectual development. Genes give a person a basic amount of raw material to work with. Circumstances often determine how that raw material develops.

Often a specific talent will run in a family. The Bach family produced many talented musicians, and the Breughel family produced a lot of painters. Mathematical ability also appears to be transmitted genetically.

Just as a certain amount of intelligence can be inherited, so can a variety of metabolic disorders and imbalances in enzymes of the brain. There are now tests for many of these problems, and some of them can be treated through diet regulation.

Some hereditary problems are tied to the sex chromosome. Often these are recessive traits. A famous example of this is the emergence of hemophilia in Queen Victoria's family. Hemophilia affects only male children. Women carry the recessive gene, but never develop the disease.

The diagram below shows how this disease is transmitted genetically. The mother carries the undesirable gene, called X. Of the four offspring, one boy and one girl will not carry the gene to the next generation. One boy will develop hemophilia and one girl will carry the gene. When she marries, two out of four children could inherit the undesirable gene. If one of the children inheriting the gene is a male, he will develop hemophilia, because there is no healthy X gene that will dominate the unhealthy X gene. Hereditary diseases are not usually linked with the Y gene.

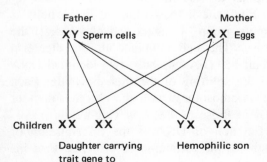

Father
X Y Sperm cells

Mother
X X Eggs

Children X X   X X   Y X   Y X

Daughter carrying
trait gene to
next generation

Hemophilic son

Chromosomes carrying the hemophilic trait are carried by the mother. (Affected chromosomes are circled.)

Transmission of Hereditary Patterns

We now know that chromosomes and genes determine traits of heredity. But how, we may ask, does this happen? To answer this question, we must delve into one of the many amazing aspects of creation. At one point or another, all people have gazed into the star-speckled night and marveled at the immensity of the universe. Our minds cannot comprehend the dimensions of the world of which we are a part. The mechanisms of heredity are no less amazing than the scope of the universe. Imagine the possibility of looking into yourself and seeing the elements that make up your being. Of course, to examine them, you would have to be able to see on the molecular level.

Chromosomes are basically made up of a chemical called deoxyribonucleic acid, or DNA. The helix structure of DNA resembles a circular staircase. The sides of the staircase are made up of sugars and phosphorus. The steps are made up of chemicals called bases. Each step is composed of two bases. There are four different bases: adenine, thymine, guanine, and cytosine. Adenine and thymine always join to form a step, and guanine and cytosine always pair off to form a step.

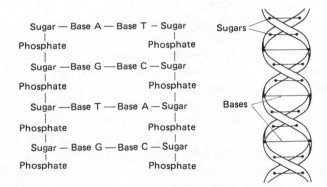

The diagram will help us to visualize how chromosomes regroup during cell division. First, the helixes separate. Each helix is then made up of only a single group of sugars and phosphates; the half bars are only one base. The cell contains all the elements necessary to complete the half helix. As a result, two identical DNA molecules are a product of the splitting of the first molecule. Each cell division results in two chromosomes, with the chromosomes of the first cell being identical to those of the new cell.

The most important function of DNA is the transmission of information to the cytoplasm for the formation of proteins. Proteins

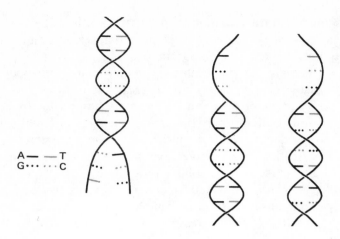

A— —T
G··· ···C

are made up of amino acids linked to one another. DNA is locked
in the nucleus of the cell. For the information to be transmitted to
the cytoplasm, a type of messenger must be sent out. This messenger is called ribonucleic acid (RNA). RNA can be thought of as
a negative of the DNA strand. Each point on the DNA helix
corresponds to a point on the RNA molecule. RNA is made up of
the same bases as DNA, except that uracile replaces thymine. These
bases are grouped into triplets; for example, guanine-guanine-
guanine would be GGG. Other triplets might be GUU, GGU, or
ACA. The triplets are a code for what is needed by the DNA
molecule. When the RNA enters the cytoplasm of the cell, ribo-
somes attach themselves to the extremities of the triplets and find
out what compounds are needed. The necessary amino acids are
linked together until the protein dictated by the DNA is formed.

The genetic code is a fundamental element of our being. All
cells contain the same set of genes and chromosomes. Theoretically,
one cell could fabricate the whole organism, because the possibilities for combinations number in the millions. To regulate cell
growth, some genes fabricate proteins that repress random cellular
growth. In this way the correct cells are made for each organ. The
combination of genes that require growth proteins and those that
require repressive proteins causes an automatic regulation of cellular
growth.

Mutations

Altered genes do not function correctly; a mutation occurs.
Mutations can be good or bad, serious or of no importance. They
are unforeseeable, unalterable, and occur completely by chance. If

the mutation occurs in a dominant gene, the result will show up in the second generation. If the affected gene is recessive, the mutation may not show up for several generations.

The mutation can be completely spontaneous or happen as a result of outside causes. Many mutations result from natural radioactivity. The surface of the earth is constantly bombarded by cosmic rays. A person receives approximately 3 roentgens of radioactivity during the reproductive years from these rays and radiation from the earth itself. Artificial radioactive rays can be received from many sources in the course of a person's reproductive years. Too many X-rays can be dangerous. The total number of X-rays received by the average person during a lifetime doubles the amount of radiation received naturally. For this reason, X-rays should be held to a minimum.

Mutations happen when an error takes place in the base of a DNA molecule. The loss of a fragment of DNA interrupts the chaining of amino acids together. The results can be grave. For example, in the development of hemoglobin, a substitution of one of a series of 300 amino acids results in serious forms of anemia, such as sickle-cell anemia.

ADAPTATION OF THE BODY TO PREGNANCY

Pregnancy is a perfectly normal state. However, the body must make many adjustments to accommodate itself to the new state. From the very beginning the body undergoes tremendous hormonal changes. Gonadotropic hormones are secreted by the placenta. The corpus luteum secretes significant quantities of estrogens and progesterones during the first three months. These hormones affect the different body organs and the nervous system.

For this reason, the first stage of pregnancy may give the future mother problems, and it may be difficult for her to adapt herself in all the necessary ways. Physical and psychological adjustments must take place.

Many physical changes will occur, the most obvious being the enlargement of the uterus. Gradually, the uterus will displace the surrounding organs. The functions of these organs are modified by pregnancy. Changes occur in all parts of the body. Blood thickens, the heartbeat increases by 30%, and the volume of blood increases. The kidneys must work harder; breathing becomes stronger; the liver is more active. The tissues of the body retain more water than normal during pregnancy. These changes occur during the first trimester.

During the second trimester the mother has adjusted to many of these changes. Most of the unpleasant side effects (nausea and the like) have tapered off. The second trimester is usually a peaceful time for the mother.

During the third trimester, the body prepares for childbirth. (We review this in more detail later.) The placenta has stopped growing, the gonadotropic hormones and the estrogens diminish little by little, and the permeability of the placenta diminishes. A full return to the nonpregnant state won't be complete until several weeks after delivery.

2

Pregnancy is a natural state. During this century, most pregnancies have become problem free, but in the past, this was not always the case. Many situations arose that were serious for both mother and child. Today, having a child is usually very safe.

During the last 20 years medicine has developed techniques for the surveillance of each stage of pregnancy. The reason for this is not only to prevent accidents but to spot problems as early as possible and to resolve them. The rate of problems is five times higher among newborns whose mothers have had no prenatal care, and 60% more difficulties are noted among mothers who have had no prenatal care. Four visits are considered essential, but one should really see the physician once a month, with more frequent visits toward the end of the pregnancy.

THE FIRST CONSULTATION

Am I Pregnant?

You think that you may be pregnant, and for this reason you go to your doctor to find out for sure. The first sign that you may be pregnant might be missing your monthly period. Even among women who have regular cycles, being a few days late does not always mean that a pregnancy is in progress. A period can be delayed for many reasons: fatigue, anemia, sickness, stress, or nervous shock. However, a missed period may be a sign of pregnancy.

Other signs can occur in the beginning of a pregnancy. The

What Will Happen During Your Pregnancy?

best known is nausea, or morning sickness. Usually this comes on quickly and can be provoked by certain odors, such as coffee, cigarette smoke, or perfume. Often, a woman notices a change in her appetite; her tastes for foods may be different than normal, and salivation may increase. Urination may become more frequent, forcing her to get up more often during the night. Some people have a desire to sleep more than usual. Some are nervous for no apparent reason. For women who keep track of temperature changes during their cycles, their temperature stays slightly higher than normal on the twenty-eighth day of the cycle instead if dipping. Each person reacts somewhat differently.

However, the most frequent sign is the lack of a period, and it is at this time that most women consult a doctor. It could be that this will be your first gynecological exam. If so, you may feel a certain apprehension. In fact, these examinations are not painful and will go more smoothly if you are relaxed. The doctor wants to find out if all the internal organs are correctly placed and if the volume of your uterus has changed. Before pregnancy, your uterus is ovoid, and during pregnancy it becomes rounder and softer. Included in the examination is a general physical and tests that are covered in greater detail further on in the chapter. If you are very thin and have supple abdominal muscles, it may be possible to detect pregnancy by an internal exam alone. Usually the doctor cannot detect a pregnancy by examination alone before the sixth week.

If you are heavier than normal, if your abdominal muscles are resistant to pressure, or if your womb tips toward the back, it may be difficult to tell if you are pregnant even at six weeks. The doctor may not notice an increase in the volume of your uterus for another 10 or 15 days.

Lab Tests for Pregnancy

To determine if a woman is pregnant before physical signs develop, a clinical test is necessary. In the past the Friedman test was often used. Urine from the woman was injected into a female rabbit over a two-day period. On the third day, the rabbit was killed, and the ovaries inspected. If the animal's ovaries showed signs of pregnancy, the test was positive, because hormones in the woman's urine had caused the animal to show signs of pregnancy. This test is 97% accurate but is not widely used today, because of the time and money involved.

Blood tests are frequently used today. Blood is drawn and

tested for the presence of HCG (human chorionic gonadotrophin). The HCG-receptor assay test has an accuracy rate of 97.4 percent; however, the test can also yield a 2.3 percent incidence of false-positive reactions. Another is called the HCG beta-subunit test. Both procedures involve measuring secretions of the endocrine system, or hormones, that are released into the bloodstream during pregnancy.

As mentioned in Chapter 1, simpler, faster tests have been developed. (One can even buy kits to test for pregnancy at a drugstore. These tests cannot replace a medical consultation, though.) The test reacts positively because the trophoblast blastocyst (fertilized ovum) secretes hormones that show up in the woman's urine. One can not be sure of a positive reaction before the sixth day after the missed period. Before this time, a negative result can take place, even though a pregnancy is in progress. If legal questions are involved, a second test should be made eight days after the first test to remove all doubts.

Once pregnancy is confirmed, your physician will take a personal medical history. Questions will be asked about your family, your parents' families, and your husband's family. This step gives the physician important information that may answer questions arising at a later date. A more complete physical examination may also be given at this point. Any illnesses that existed before the pregnancy must be dealt with. All these procedures are a routine part of a pregnant woman's medical care.

Routine Lab Tests

Certain tests are necessary.

A blood test is performed to rule out the presence of syphilis.

A test is made to determine your blood type. You know that there are four principal blood groups: A, B, AB, and O. You will also be tested for a positive or negative Rh factor. If you are Rh negative and your husband is Rh positive, tests will have to be made to find out if there are antibodies and antigens present.

Your urine is checked for sugar or albumin. If either of these substances is present, further tests must be performed.

Unless there is a serious reason for it, no X-rays are performed. A lung X-ray may be done at the beginning of the sixth month.

Other tests are not obligatory but are recommended. Among these are a rubella test and a toxoplasmosis test.

When Will the Child Be Born?

The duration of the usual pregnancy is about 280 days, or 9 months and 10 days. You can calculate your date of delivery easily. Simply take the first day of your last period, for example, January 1, add 10 days; this would give you January 11. Subtract 3 months, December, November, and October. Your baby will be born around October 11.

What Should I Expect
in the Beginning of My Pregnancy?

Although pregnancy is not a sickness, certain precautions should be observed. The most important guideline is to lead a normal life without excesses of any sort.

The first three months of pregnancy are a period of adaptation for your body. Certain functional problems, mainly digestive, may occur. Nausea varies from person to person. Sometimes it occurs in the morning and does not return until the next morning. Some people leave the table to vomit, then return to finish the meal. Certain foods upset some people.

It is recommended that several small meals be eaten during the day. Have a small breakfast upon arising, or even before getting up. Lie in bed a few minutes after eating, to help avoid upset. Around ten o'clock, have a cracker with some tea. Your lunch should be light but substantial. Around four in the afternoon, have crackers and fruit, and then a light dinner. Generally these problems aren't too troublesome and disappear after the third month. Nausea can be alleviated by medication if the problem becomes too severe.

Constipation is often a problem. This can bring on headaches and assorted minor ills.

Braxton Hick's Contractions Some time after the third month, Braxton Hick's contractions begin. These are usually painless sensations of squeezing or pulling in the uterus. They occur infrequently and irregularly except late in pregnancy, when they may be experienced at ten- or twenty-minute intervals and may create some discomfort. They are quite normal and are not the contractions of labor.

Personal Hygiene It is important to maintain a regular program of personal hygiene during pregnancy. Take baths, but make sure that the water is not too hot or too cold. It should be about body temperature. Don't lock yourself in the bathroom, and try to avoid bathing if you are alone in the house.

You should brush your teeth carefully after each meal. Some women's gums may be prone to bleeding. This makes your choice of toothpaste more serious than you might think, because some may be too abrasive. Your dentist can advise you on this. If any abnormality shows up in your teeth or gums, you should see your dentist. Contrary to popular opinion, dental treatments are safe during pregnancy. Any dental needs should be attended to.

Cleansing of your genitals should be done with your normal soap. Douching is not recommended during pregnancy, but if it is desired, use a device that circulates the cleansing fluid gently (avoid high-pressure devices such as bulb syringes).

Dressing During the Early Months of Pregnancy At the very beginning of pregnancy, there are few problems in wearing your normal wardrobe. As you grow larger, more roomy clothes will be more comfortable. Many stores carry comfortable, stylish clothes for the pregnant woman. As you grow, special undergarments can help support the additional weight. Your regular bra will be sufficient in the beginning. Later a bra with more support may be necessary, to prevent your breasts from stretching from the extra weight and volume. Some doctors suggest special night wear; your doctor will advise you on this. The choice of shoes is very important. High heels are not appropriate as the pregnancy progresses, because they accentuate the increased arch in the back that results from pregnancy. They also increase the chances of falling and injuring yourself and the baby. Flat shoes may not support the foot and arch adequately, either. Heels of a midheight often give the best support. They should be somewhat larger in size than normal to accommodate any swelling of the feet.

Your Lifestyle Doing your normal amount of work is recommended, but you should avoid large undertakings and tasks that are not necessary. Don't lift heavy objects, carry objects that are unevenly weighted, or rearrange heavy furniture. If you work outside the home, you can stay on your job as long as you and your doctor feel it is advisable. Any abnormalities (extreme sickness, fatigue, or blood flow) mean that you should probably not continue working. Certain circumstances (doing heavy work, change in the length of hours) may necessitate a change in position, but this is not always possible. In these cases, you and your doctor should assess the situation together. A leave of absence may be in order.

You may continue with your favorite sports, as long as they are not violent in nature. Horseback riding, skiing, and diving are among the sports that are not generally recommended. Later on, most sports will be prohibited to avoid shocks and jolts to the uterus. One activity that you can do until the end of your pregnancy is walking, as long as it does not tire you too much. Swimming is fine, as long as you don't stay in too long and avoid violent movements.

Smoking is not advised, but if you are not able to give up this habit, try not to smoke more than 10 cigarettes a day. Smoking can result in many problems, both to you and to your baby.

Drinking of alcohol is strongly advised against. Also, be extremely cautious about medications that contain sedatives. These drugs may affect the developing fetus.

Traveling in the beginning of a pregnancy is fine as long as the means of travel are not too rugged. If you are experiencing extreme sickness or bleeding, travel should be avoided unless absolutely necessary.

Sexual Relations During Pregnancy

Much controversy exists on the question of sexual relations during pregnancy. There have been few scientific studies on the subject, and as a result, many hold diverse opinions. Some cultural attitudes toward motherhood, coupled with the taboos that many people feel about sexuality as a whole, have colored the situation even more. These notions show an ignorance of biological realities. A better understanding of the circumstances surrounding procreation helps to dispel fears about the subject.

During pregnancy, sexual desire may be in a state of change because of the hormonal changes that occur. Some note an increase in sexual desire, others a lessening. Often, there is no noticeable change.

During the first trimester the state of the uterus is about the same as before the pregnancy. The uterus is quite flexible during this time.

Generally, sexual activity is safe during pregnancy. However, a woman with a history of miscarriage may want to avoid intercourse during the period when the miscarriages occurred. Any women who have experienced vaginal bleeding or whose membranes have ruptured should not have intercourse in order to prevent infection. An increased risk of infection also exists during the last month of pregnancy, when the cervix has begun to dilate.

During the last trimester the cervix may be shortened. Uterine contractions are more frequent, and the fetus may have dropped. Some doctors think that sexual intercourse may start premature contractions. Others argue that sexual activity causes about the same conditions that already exist in the womb, because the body is preparing for labor, and contractions take place regularly anyway. The volume of the uterus and the relative weakness of abdominal muscles help to protect the fetus from a premature delivery or miscarriage.

In conclusion, each woman and her mate must assess their own situation in light of their preferences. If medical problems are involved, a doctor's opinion should be sought.

MEDICATIONS, VACCINES, AND ILLNESSES

The side effects of thalidomide on unborn children have alerted the public and the medical community to the dangers of medication to unborn children.

Pharmaceutical laboratories perform experiments on animals (e.g., rats, rabbits, and guinea pigs) to find out if any side effects will occur. However, one cannot be sure that a drug will have the same effect on human beings. For this reason, doctors do not prescribe new drugs for pregnant women unless the situation is so grave that trying a new drug is the only option. Even with medications that are known to be harmless, doctors do not prescribe them unless they can be completely passed through the digestive system. You should never take any type of medication, even if you think it's harmless, without consulting your doctor. Take only drugs that have been prescribed by your doctor.

Problems with vaccinations rarely occur during pregnancy. If, for some reason, you had to take a trip to Africa or Central America, a vaccine against cholera could be taken, but not against yellow fever. Only a dead virus may be taken, not the live version of a vaccine. Antitetanus, antirabies, and antidiphtherial vaccines may be taken.

Two sicknesses, rubella and toxoplasmosis, have extremely serious consequences for the unborn child. About 90% of the female population is protected from rubella, having contracted it in their childhood. Antibodies against rubella (or German measles) are present in their bloodstream. For the 10% who are not immune to the disease, contact with anyone having the disease must be avoided.

With toxoplasmosis, as well, 90% of the population is immune, but 10% could catch the disease. A parasite causes the disease, but doctors do not know how. Cats sometimes carry the parasite. The parasite is found in raw meat and on the surface of fruits and vegetables. If your toxoplasmosis test shows negative results, make sure that your meat is well cooked, carefully clean all fruits and vegetables, and avoid cats. (For a more specific discussion of the problem of illnesses in pregnancy, see Chapter 4.)

Chronic Sickness in the Pregnant Woman

In the past, diabetes, tuberculosis, and heart problems all posed serious problems for the pregnant woman. Today, thanks to advances in treatment, a pregnancy can go to term if the woman is closely watched by a doctor. Each case poses particular problems, and you should consult your doctor if you are in this situation.

YOU AND YOUR DOCTOR

You should see your doctor when you first think that you are pregnant and set up a schedule for the subsequent months. Although visits every few months are essential, most doctors recommend a visit at the beginning of each month. As we have mentioned, visits at regular intervals reduce prenatal problems significantly.

If you notice any abnormality, you should see your physician. Be particularly alert to these symptoms: a passage of any amount of blood (note if it is red or blackish in color), any unusual abdominal pains (particularly if they are rhythmic), unusually heavy vomiting or painful urination.

When you see your doctor, it is a good idea to have your observations written down so that you don't forget anything.

AFTER THE FIRST CONSULTATION

Your Diet

As you speak to various people, you will encounter two schools of thought on the subject of nutrition and pregnancy. Some of your friends will relate how they spent the last 4 or 5 months of their pregnancy on strict diets, to emerge as slender as they were

TABLE 2.1

Circumstances That Warrant a Doctor's Immediate Attention

Symptom	Potential Danger	Possible Solutions
Pain in the lower abdomen	*First month*: risk of miscarriage *Last trimester*: danger of premature delivery	
Bleeding	*First trimester*: risk of miscarriage, extra-uterine pregnancy, hydatidiform mole *Last trimester*: placenta previa, separation of the placenta	If the bleeding is severe, hospitalization is necessary.
Violent, persistent headaches Visual problems, dizziness, marked swelling of the legs and face	High blood pressure, toxemia pre-eclampsia	
Contact with a person with rubella	Risk of infection and fetal damage	

TABLE 2.2

Less Urgent Circumstances That Warrant a Doctor's Attention

Symptom	Potential Danger	Possible Solutions
Excessive weight gain	Possible beginning of toxemia and resulting complications (eclampsia, etc.)	Rest, cut down on salt, diet
Albumin in the urine	Same as above	Rest, lower salt intake
Regular headaches	Same as above	Rest, lower salt intake
Excessive need to urinate, burning urination	Urinary infection	Urine analysis and visual examination of the vulva and anti-microbial treatment
Vaginal discharge of white or greenish pus	Genital infection	Analysis of the discharge and treatment

before they became pregnant. Others will tell you that you are eating for two now and that your intake of food should reflect this.

Actually, your diet does concern two people. You often feel hungry, but you don't want to gain too much weight. Your baby draws every element that is needed from your body and from your food intake.

In the past, eating for two often left slender young women obese after one or two pregnancies. Also, extra pounds do not make labor and delivery easier.

During our time, considerations for fashion have resulted in diets that are too strict. Fetal malnutrition has resulted, in some cases, comparable to that seen in times of famine or malnutrition. The sensible course lies in the middle of these two extremes.

What Are Your Nutritional Needs?   The body experiences a loss of energy every moment. Energy is needed to maintain muscular functions, to keep body temperature at 98.6°F, for respiratory functions, and for the numerous chemical functions that take place in our organs. These energy needs are measured in calories.

To compensate for these energy losses, we eat food. Food furnishes the body with calories. The quantity of calories is determined by age, weight, and physical activity. A young woman weighing 130 pounds and having a light amount of physical activity needs about 2000 calories per day. The diet should be well balanced, consisting of proteins, carbohydrates, and fats.

Proteins are the essential components of the cell. One can compare them to the bricks in a building. They ensure the construction and maintenance of the organs, and they participate in the formation of the enzymes necessary for life. The carbohydrates give the body fuel to burn. They are energy foods. Fats are indispensable because they carry certain vitamins through the system.

During pregnancy, your food intake requirements increase by 20%. Thus you will probably need about 2500 calories a day, more if you work outside the home. If you are nursing, you need about 3000 calories a day. A high percentage of this diet should be proteins. An increase in minerals and sugars is needed, as is an increase in iron. Vitamins C and D should also be increased.

To ensure a nutritious diet, be sure to increase intake of these foods: meats, fish, and eggs as protein sources; green vegetables, liver, and fruits as vitamin and iron sources; and cheeses and milk products, which supply phosphorous and calcium. This type of diet is varied, balanced, and adapted to give you the elements you and your unborn child need. Look closely at the foods you are now eating to see if they are nutritionally sound.

Lean meats are recommended. Beef contains 165 calories for each 100 grams, with 18 grams of protein and 10 grams of fat. Veal and lamb also have these proportions of protein and fat. Chicken has 150 calories per 100 grams, 20 grams of which are protein. Pregnant women are advised to avoid sausage products. Ham that is well cooked and trimmed of fat may also be eaten. Lean fish average about 80 calories per 100 grams and have about 16 grams of protein and very little fat. Meats that don't have a high protein/fat ratio should be avoided. Pork, for example, is very high in fat and calories. Canned and artificially preserved meats should be avoided. Duck and turkey contain more fat than chicken and should be avoided. Marinated and spicy meats should not be eaten. Fatty fishes, such as sardines and mackerel, and smoked fish, caviar, shellfish, and snails should also be avoided.

Milk is almost a complete food. It contains protein, fats, calcium, phosphorous, and vitamins and minerals. At least 1 quart of milk should be drunk daily. It can be included in sauces and with other foods.

Milk is not easily digested by everyone. It can cause gas, prolonged digestion, and intestinal troubles. For people who have trouble drinking milk, cheese is a good substitute. Cheeses are very nourishing, but should not be eaten in large quantities because they are high in fats and salts.

Green vegetables and salads are rich in vitamins. Carrots and spinach contain minerals and iron. Salad greens are rich in vitamin C, as are beets and tomatoes. These vegetables also help to fight constipation. Some vegetables are more difficult to digest than others. These include cabbage, kidney beans, and peas.

Prolonged cooking destroys vitamins. For this reason do not overcook vegetables. Cooking with a vegetable steamer helps to keep the vitamins in. The closer a vegetable is to its natural state, the higher the vitamin content will be.

All fresh fruit is good to eat because it is rich in vitamin C. Pineapple, lemons, strawberries, raspberries, currants, melons, oranges, and grapefruit are particularly high in vitamin C. Fruits that are not as high in vitamin C include peaches, pears, apples, and apricots.

Dried fruits are not recommended.

Bread, biscuits, pastry, cereals, and potatoes are sources of carbohydrates and are very high in calories. Sugar is a high-energy food, but should be taken in moderate amounts.

Small amounts of oil are nutritionally sound, and fresh butter is also good.

Although small amounts of wine are not harmful, liqueurs, aperitifs, and hard liquor are not recommended, except occasionally.

One or two cups of tea or coffee a day are acceptable. Enough water should be drunk to keep your kidneys functioning well.

Summary Food Lists

FOODS THAT SHOULD BE EATEN

Lean meats: beef, veal, lamb (without fat), liver (once a week)
Chicken
Smoked meats: ham trimmed of fat
Lean fish: whiting, sole, cod, trout
Cheese: nonfermented cheese
Eggs
Fruits (fresh and well ripened): pineapple, raspberries, lemons, strawberries, currants, melons, grapefruit, grapes
Vegetables: tomatoes, spinach, salad greens, beets (cabbage and peas can sometimes cause gas)
Starches (do not eat in excess, because you'll gain weight): potatoes, bread
Beverages: water, tea, coffee, small amounts of wine
Seasonings: herbs

FOODS THAT SHOULD BE AVOIDED

Fatty meats: pork, gravies, canned meats
Fatty poultry: duck, turkey
Smoked meats and sausages (avoid everything except ham)
Cheeses: fermented cheese, Roquefort, Camembert
Nuts
Dry vegetables
Starches: biscuits, pastry, French fries, cake, excessive sweets
Beverages: alcoholic beverages
Seasonings: hot spices, mayonnaise

IDEAL DAILY DIET

Milk	1 qt.
Cheese	2 oz.
Broiled or roasted meat	8–12 oz.
Butter	1 oz.
Olive oil	1½ oz.
Fruit (cooked or fresh)	16–20 oz.
Potatoes	8 oz.
Bread	8 oz.
Sugar	6 tsp.

6 oz. meat = 12 oz. lean fish = 2 fresh eggs = 1 slice of ham
8 oz. potatoes = 2½ oz. of rice = 2 oz. dried peas
2 oz. cheese = 2 servings of yogurt = 4 oz. milk

MENU SUGGESTIONS

Breakfast: Coffee or tea with milk, bread, butter, jelly, one fruit or juice.
Lunch: Salad, meat or meat equivalent, green vegetable, cheese.
At 4 PM, if you are hungry, you may have an apple or yogurt.
Dinner: Vegetable soup; meat, eggs, or fish; green vegetables; fruit. Twice a week you may have liver, lentils, spinach greens, or kidney beans.

MENU FOR MILK AND MILK SUBSTITUTES

Milk (for a person who digests milk well)
Breakfast: 1 glass of milk, bread with butter, jam.
Lunch: Tomato salad, potatoes, grilled meat, cheese, 1 fruit.
Afternoon snack: 1 yogurt.
Dinner: Vegetable soup, ham, greens with butter, apple, milk.
Milk Substitute Menu
Breakfast: Bread and cheese, well ripened piece of fruit.
Lunch: Vegetable, fish, potatoes with butter, cheese, cherries.
Afternoon snack: Bread with cheese.
Dinner: Vegetable soup, veal, bread and butter, apricots in juice.

Practical Advice on Food Preparation

Meats should be broiled or roasted. Make sure that they are well cooked to avoid toxoplasmosis. Gravy should be avoided, because bread is usually eaten with gravy, and both are high in calories. Cooking oils are difficult to digest, and fried foods are very high in calories. If you want some fried foods, have them after having eaten something else, to avoid upset. Vegetables should be boiled or steamed. Wash them well before cooking.

These are only suggestions. Try to eat nutritiously, and avoid excessive weight gain. If you are gaining more than 2½ pounds a month, cut back on your food intake. Too many extra pounds increase the possibilities of complications during labor.

If you are gaining too much weight, your diet is probably badly regulated and contains too many carbohydrates and sugars. You should eliminate extras that have little or no nutritional value. This includes cakes, snacks, and candy. If you are experiencing hunger pains, don't eat foods that excite the appetite. Examples of this type of food are rich gravies and salted and fried foods. Don't use too much salt, and have fewer side dishes with your meals, such as biscuits and bread. Your menu should be mainly composed of meat, fish, fresh vegetables, and fruits.

CALORIE TABLE FOR LOW-CALORIE FOODS

Meat and fish (4 oz. unless otherwise indicated)

Beef	290
Liver	160
Lamb (broiled)	385
Chicken	225
Veal cutlet (broiled)	175
White fish (broiled)	125

Vegetables

Artichokes (1 lg.)	70
Asparagus (canned)	40
Carrots (1 c.)	45
Celery (1 lg. stick)	5
Mushrooms (½ c., fresh)	30
Cauliflower (1 c.)	30
Cucumber (8 in.)	15
Endive (10 inner leaves)	20
Lettuce hearts (4 oz.)	15
Green peppers (stuffed, 1 med.)	155
Onion (1 lg., raw)	50
Radishes (4 sm.)	10
Tomatoes (1 c.)	50

Fruits

Apricots (3 med.)	40
Bananas (1 med.)	95
Cherries (1 c.)	85
Strawberries (½ c., fresh)	30
Mandarin orange (1 med.)	50
Honeydew (¼ average)	65
Orange (1 med.)	70

Grapefruit (½ c., sections)	45
Peaches (1 med.)	50
Pears (1 med.)	75
Prunes (stewed, no sugar, 4 oz.)	165
Grapes (1 c.)	90
Milk products	
Cottage cheese (½ c.)	65
Skim milk (1 c.)	85
Yogurt (1 c.)	150
Eggs (1 med.)	80
Butter (1 tbsp.)	100

THE SIXTH-MONTH CONSULTATION

How Is Your Pregnancy Progressing?

Between the third and fourth months, your morning sickness probably cleared up. Now your appetite is good, and you probably experience sharp hunger pangs from time to time. It is at this point in your pregnancy that you are likely to gain unwanted pounds. You should gain about 2 pounds per month from here on.

By now, you have begun to "show" your pregnancy. Usually this occurs during the fourth month. One can gauge your growth by measuring the distance from your pubic bone to the top of the uterus. At 3 months, this distance measures about 3½ inches. By 4 months, it is about 6½ inches. By 4½ months, uterine growth

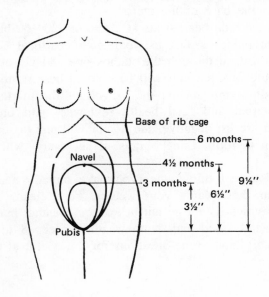

reaches your navel; by 5 months, the distance measures about 8 inches; and by 6 months, it is 9½ inches. These measurements vary from person to person.

From the side, you may still look more or less the same. Some women don't look pregnant until the last few months. Others look pregnant much sooner. Perhaps the abdominal muscles are not strong, or the uterus might be tipped to the front. Usually, though, women's abdominal muscles are quite strong, and their circulation in this area is good.

Movements of the Fetus   The first movements are usually noticed at 4½ months. They are usually quite small and could be mistaken for digestive movements. Women who have had several children recognize these first movements more quickly than first-time mothers. Sometimes the mother doesn't notice anything until late in the pregnancy. As the pregnancy continues, the movements become more vigorous. Sometimes the fetus is restless for a period of time, then is calm for a while. Often it seems that the fetus starts moving around just as you are ready to go to bed, after being quiet all day.

If you don't feel the baby moving at 4½ months, don't panic. Some mothers don't notice any movement until the sixth month, or even later. A lot depends on the baby and on the thickness of tissues between you and the baby.

However, if you have felt regular movement and suddenly don't notice any, you should contact your doctor immediately.

At 6 months, the fetal head is at the top of your uterus. At some point during the next 3 months, the baby will probably turn, so that the head is in the base of the uterus.

By 4½ months, the fetal heart beats at a rate of 120–160 beats per minute, which is twice as fast as your own heartbeat. The doctor can hear the heartbeat through the stethoscope and via ultra-sound, and with a little practice you will be able to hear it, too.

During your visit to the doctor, the growth of the uterus is verified, general maternal and fetal health reviewed, and blood pressure taken. If you are Rh negative, the doctor will test to see if antibodies have begun to form. Lung X-rays, if necessary, will be taken at this time.

The doctor will repeat things that you have already heard, mainly to watch your diet, watch your weight, keep clean, and avoid unnecessary activities. Don't go out in extreme weather inadequately clothed, especially cold and damp weather. Sleep 8 to 10 hours. You will probably have some questions for the doctor at this point.

The Maternity Girdle The role of a maternity girdle is to support the uterus. Normally, the abdominal muscles are adequate for this purpose. However, if you are experiencing tearing of the abdominal muscles, kidney or bladder problems, or muscle weaknesses resulting from previous pregnancies, a maternity girdle might be a good idea.

There is a simple method to ascertain if you need one. Interlock your fingers over your abdomen, and lift the uterus slightly. This is exactly what a correctly fitted girdle will do, because it should lift slightly without creasing the abdomen. If this test alleviates distress, you might need a maternity girdle. You can probably judge this better than your doctor. Try on several before buying. Make sure that it is not too tight and doesn't leave a crease on the abdomen.

Stretch Marks Stretch marks are small, thin, rose-colored lines that may appear on the abdomen, hips, and breasts. After pregnancy, they will turn ivory colored. By applying creams to the areas mentioned above, you can minimize these lines. Cocoa butter and olive oil are recommended. The best way to minimize stretch marks is to avoid putting on too much weight. If the abdomen becomes too large, wearing a maternity girdle will help.

The Mask of Pregnancy (Chloasma) This may occur during a pregnancy. Dark-haired people are more prone to this. The face has small, coffee-colored blotches on the forehead and temples. The markings disappear after pregnancy. To minimize them you should stay out of the sun or use a sun-blocking cream. Makeup and soap will not improve this condition significantly. Pigmentation will also increase around the nipple of the breast. On the abdomen, one may notice a brown line extending from the navel to the pubis. This also disappears or fades after delivery.

THE EIGHTH-MONTH VISIT

Your abdomen has increased in volume. At 7 months, the uterus measures around 10½ inches. At 8 months the uterus has grown to 12 inches. These measurements vary from person to person, so don't be alarmed if you are bigger or smaller. The most important fact is that you have grown and that a heartbeat can be heard. You are very aware of fetal activity during these last months. Occasionally, you will experience a kick or a small punch. Movement seems to be

everywhere, and you may wonder if you have twins! Some people notice more movement on one side than the other. Usually this means that the arms and legs are on one side of the uterus and the back on the other. The fetus may not move for long periods of time. If a time passes when there seems to be no movement, you should call your doctor. Some women don't notice movement until late in the pregnancy, and even then the child is not very active.

Until this time, the fetus has been in a sort of "seated" position, the head being at the top of the uterus. Around the seventh or eighth month, the fetus will turn, and the head will be in the base of your pelvis. When this happens, you will be able to feel the baby's head by placing your hand at the base of your uterus. The seat of the baby is by your liver, and you can see it as an irregular form. Between the two, you can see the back on either your right or left side. Contractions also occur from time to time, and the uterus may seem hard at certain times.

You should not gain more than 2½ pounds per month during these last months. You may notice kidney pains and a shifting of the pubic bone or the sacral triangle. Occasionally, this discomfort may hit a large nerve, and you'll experience pain, but this is quite rare. The entire pelvic area retains a lot of fluid (in order to remain elastic), so most relaxation of the ligaments supporting the bones and organs is not painful.

Because the uterus is so high, the other organs must rearrange themselves around it. You may notice pains in your sides that are more or less persistent. Some people feel that the baby is lying on the liver. This area is very sensitive during these last months. Some experience mild discomfort when breathing heavily, for example, when going up stairs. These problems are not serious and occur less frequently in women who have had natural-childbirth classes.

Other discomforts include leg cramps (often resulting from circulatory problems or a lack of calcium) or a burning in the stomach. The sensation may be noticed along the esophagus and in the throat. You may notice this when lying down, and it disappears when you get up. If the problem is severe, medication can be prescribed to alleviate it.

It is very important to be in touch with your doctor and to have regular visits every two weeks. Your urine should be tested for albumin regularly. If your feet are swollen and your rings don't fit, you are retaining too much water. Cut back on your salt intake during these last two months to cut water retention. Excessive water retention makes labor more difficult.

Sexual activity should be quite moderate during this time. You may want to leave your job if you are working outside the home. Begin to think of preparations for your hospital stay. Find out what items you will need. Your labor may start sooner than you think, and it would be easy to forget a critical item in the rush to the hospital.

THE NINTH-MONTH VISIT

As with the previous visits, your urine will be checked, along with your blood pressure, heartbeat, and the fetus's heartbeat. Your diet will be reviewed.

Your uterus has lengthened to between 12½ to 13½ inches. The baby continues to move, and from time to time you feel a contraction. The baby now weighs 6 pounds or more.

The fetus is now in a position to be born. This position is called the presentation. The most common presentation (95%) is with the head of the fetus turned toward the back, with the chin resting on the chest. The face turned toward the back of the uterus is an excellent position for easy passage and is one sign of a happy labor.

The left, anterior, occipital presentation is the most common and favorable presentation. The right, posterior, occipital presentation is less frequent but is also favorable.

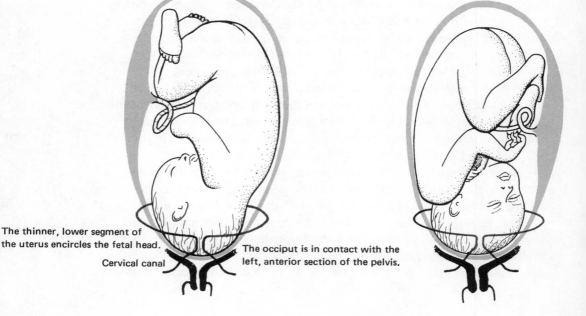

The thinner, lower segment of the uterus encircles the fetal head.

Cervical canal

The occiput is in contact with the left, anterior section of the pelvis.

The head of the fetus is bent slightly and rests at the top of the vagina just before birth. Most often, the occipital part of the head is the lowermost part of the baby's body. The baby's body is usually turned slightly to the left. This is called a longitudinal presentation. Occasionally, the fetus is turned slightly to the right, instead of to the left. This is also a good presentation for labor. For the widest part of the head to pass the lower section of the uterus, the baby descends into the true pelvic area. When this happens, the head is engaged.

Ultrasound techniques can be used to examine the fetus, without danger to the fetus or to the mother. High-frequency sound waves are bounced off the fetus and back onto a screen. Various abnormalities, particularly those of position, can be discovered by means of this technique. It is possible to measure the fetal head to within 1 or 2 millimeters.

In women who are having their first child, the head becomes engaged a few weeks before delivery, usually by the eighth-month office visit. However, don't be disturbed if this hasn't occurred at this time. It will probably happen during the next few weeks. If it doesn't happen before you go into labor, your doctor may have to take some extra precautions. The engagement takes place later in women who have had children before. Sometimes it does not happen until immediately before labor.

WAITING FOR THE DELIVERY

Now, there is nothing to be done but to wait until the delivery day. Try not to be impatient. For many women the last few days seem interminable. There are a few physical signs for which you should be on the alert.

Three signs can signal that labor is not far off. First, uterine contractions become longer and more intense. You should not go to the hospital when these contractions begin, especially if this is your first child. Ask your doctor at what point you should go to the hospital. If you have had other children, you may want to leave earlier than you did for your first child. Second, you may notice a passage of a clear liquid. Third, a mucous plug (which may have spots of blood in it) may be passed.

If your due date comes and goes without a delivery, you shouldn't be alarmed, but you should definitely call your doctor if you haven't delivered fourteen days after the due date. In our practice we once encountered one woman who let a month pass before notifying us. She thought that the due date had been miscalculated. This was not the problem, and a sick child was finally born as a result. This is a rare case, but delayed deliveries definitely require medical attention. See page 79 for information on delayed deliveries.

PREPARATION FOR A NATURAL DELIVERY

Many women today use natural childbirth techniques, and the results are excellent. The essential element of natural childbirth is to control pain through knowledge of the body's responses. Often, ignorance causes an emotional state which makes one more susceptible to pain. If one does not know anything about childbirth, one is more likely to believe that enormous amounts of pain are inevitable. Natural childbirth does not entail hypnosis or suggestion. It is based on the principle that mental understanding of what is happening enables one to assist the physical processes and to control pain.

Two doctors pioneered this concept. First, an English doctor named Read developed his techniques, and later Lamaze developed another method. Both based their work on the influence of the emotional state of a pregnant woman on her delivery.

Childbirth without Fear

Read, an English doctor, was struck by the delivery of a young woman. She was poor and without resources, but she delivered her child in complete serenity. She said to him, "Why should this be painful? It is a natural experience." Read, who was at the beginning of his career, reflected on the woman's words.

Then he studied his other patients and noticed that they all expected that the delivery of a child would be a horrible experience. After much thought, Read decided that fear was responsible for much of the pain his patients were experiencing. He wrote several books, but they did not have much impact. His theories rested on impressions, not on evidence. He then began a program based on a confident attitude and on physical exercises. The method was systematized by 1933.

Others were also studying the problem of pain in childbirth at this time. Methods involving hypnosis and suggestion were rapidly abandoned. However, students of Pavlov proved that expectation of pain leads to actual pain in childbirth. In 1951, Lamaze evolved his own method for natural childbirth. This method is widely used today.

Brain Responses

Sensations come from our exterior world (seeing, hearing, touching) and make themselves felt on our internal organs. These impressions on our internal structures are called interoceptions. The interoceptions go to a superficial part of the cerebral cortex in the brain. This point of the brain then becomes excited. At this same point there is a zone of the brain that controls this excitement. If the excitement is controlled at this point, it diminishes. Emotional states play a very important role in controlling the reaction of the brain. If one is in a positive state of mind, pain is less than when the person is in a negative state of mind. Thus the intensity of a physical response is determined in part by the emotional state at the time the stimulus is received.

Brain Response in Childbirth

During labor, the uterus is the source of repeated contractions. These contractions stimulate the nerve endings within the muscle tissue. The nerve endings send the messages to the brain. If a person is paralyzed by fear, the zone within the brain that controls these responses does not function properly.

For many reasons we associate childbirth with pain. This notion has been perpetrated in conversation and literature. Everyone has heard accounts of deliveries where dangerous and painful interventions have been necessary. This has conditioned us to think that childbirth equals pain.

Thus when a woman goes into labor and her contractions begin, she expects them to be painful and as a result is fearful. Fear reduces the ability of the brain to control the response. In this case, uterine contractions signal pain. Because the woman expects pain, the vicious cycle of fear leading to pain and pain leading to greater fear has begun.

If childbirth is painful because everyone expects it to be, then one should be able to eliminate pain, or at least control it through conditioning. This can be done by blocking the negative responses of the brain and replacing them with a new set of conditioned responses. Natural childbirth courses do this by explaining the body's response to pain and the course of a natural delivery, and by preparing the body for childbirth through exercises. In this way, uterine contractions during labor are not a signal for pain, but a stimulus to participate in the next step of the delivery.

Natural childbirth courses usually are started at the beginning of the sixth month. A general outline of the classes follows.

The first class describes the nervous system in detail and explains why the nervous system usually responds with pain during childbirth. The second class covers the role of breathing in controlling pain. In particular, using the diaphragm muscles correctly during labor is explained. The third class teaches patients how to relax and control their muscles, especially those of the face, of the upper extremities, and of the perineum. Muscle control conserves energy during labor and maintains an equilibrium between the nervous system and contractions during childbirth.

During the fourth class, dilation of the cervix is explained. Dilation takes place during the first stage of labor (the second stage being the birth of the child). Breathing from the diaphragm is practiced, and a second technique of breathing is explained. A technique of panting rapidly is used during the actual birth of the child.

The fifth session is usually a review of the preceding classes. Beginning signals of labor and clinical procedures may also be discussed. The sixth class will cover child care, nursing, and other postnatal topics.

The course consists of theoretical aspects and physical exercises. The fathers' presence is desirable, because they provide their mates with encouragement and also coach them in the exercises. Women should practice the exercises several times each day. By doing this, they will build confidence in their ability to handle the delivery in a constructive manner.

Any woman can prepare for childbirth using this method. Even women who anticipate problems with the delivery can benefit from the course. By giving women confidence and an understanding of what is occurring, conditions for any delivery will be improved. However, a woman who is hostile to the approach or who doesn't believe that it is effective will have great difficulty benefiting from it.

The course is taught by doctors, midwives, or nurses. The instructors give practical demonstrations and keep tabs on the progress of their patients. It is vitally important that the instructors also believe in the method. They must have the patience required to assist a mother in having her child and must reject any method that would rush a mother for convenience's sake or prescribe more medication than is necessary or desired.

In addition, hospital personnel should create an atmosphere conducive to helping the mother, making sure that everything goes smoothly. They should be calm, vigilant, and attentive. Anyone who is nervous or excitable should not be in the labor or delivery rooms. The physical surroundings should also be conducive to helping the labor go smoothly.

Childbirth and Anesthesia

Some readers may receive the impression that all of this is too complicated and that the best method is to decide to deliver the child with the aid of anesthesia. Despite the tremendous progress being made in this field, there is no perfect anesthesia that can eliminate pain for the mother and pose no danger to the fetus. Also, by using anesthesia, the mother is not able to push the baby out, and the medical staff may have to extricate the child by force.

Is natural childbirth really painless? The tenets of natural childbirth hold that childbirth is normal and therefore should be painless. As expectations of pain are lessened, actual pain lessens. Women in childbirth are much calmer now than in the past, but that is not to say that no one experiences pain anymore. The number of women who experience childbirth without pain has increased dramatically, though. Since the beginning of our practice in 1954, we have kept records on occurrences of pain between women who were prepared for childbirth and those who were not. Among the women who were prepared, 70% did not experience a great amount of pain, 20% experienced a moderate amount of pain, and 10% experienced a lot of pain. Among the women who had no preparation for childbirth, 70% experienced a lot of pain, 20% experienced a moderate amount of pain, and 10% did not have significant pain.

How much of this pain is a result of expectations? It is difficult to say. Simply admitting the possibility of pain raises the expectation for pain, which in turn can add to any pain being experienced. By approaching the same amount of pain in a positive manner, it is possible to diminish it.

The success of natural childbirth techniques proves beyond a doubt that knowledge of the role of the nervous system, the structure of the genitals, and the development of the child improves the chances for a satisfying delivery. This knowledge and preparation of the body through exercises make the whole process much easier. The exercises ensure that maximum oxygen will get to the child during childbirth. Natural childbirth techniques also strengthen the bond between the mother and those around her during delivery, the medical staff and, most of all, her husband. All these factors give the woman confidence and an important sense of security.

In conclusion, giving birth can take place with joy and pride, without the use of sense-dulling pain killers.

PHYSICAL EXERCISES IN NATURAL CHILDBIRTH

The exercises outlined here are covered in six classes in the course, which you should begin during your sixth month. Adequate preparation involves learning the facts. A progressive unfolding of information and learning through repetition ensures that everything will be covered. Usually the course is taught in small groups. You will learn a great deal in this course, but for it to be effective, you must practice daily in your home. By doing the exercises daily, you will prepare your mind and body.

These exercises should be relaxing. Any clothing you find comfortable will be fine. In the beginning, exercise for a few minutes four or five times a day. Slowly build up to the point where you can exercise for 10 minutes or so without fatigue. There are two types of exercises: respiratory exercises and exercises that help you to control neuromuscular functions.

The Respiratory Exercises

Respiratory exercises are very important to the program, because they ensure that there will be enough oxygen for both mother and child during delivery, and they enable the mother to help push the child into the world during the final stages of the delivery.

When we inhale, the rib cage expands. The diaphragm muscle is pushed outward to the abdomen. The inhaled air (21% of which is oxygen) provides the body with oxygen. The air that is exhaled contains carbon dioxide, which has been exchanged with oxygen in the lungs.

In the course of our daily lives our respiratory movements adapt themselves to our activities. If activity is intense, respiration is more forceful. More air is taken into the body, and the muscles surrounding the lungs and diaphragm (abdominal muscles, pectoral muscles, muscles of the upper arms) play a role in breathing. The

abdominal muscles are the most important. These muscles start at the base of the pelvis and continue up each side of the body. By using these abdominal muscles, air is exhaled with greater force, but even with maximum contraction, about ½ quart of air always stays in our lungs.

First Type of Breathing

Inhalation Breathe in through your nose, because nasal breathing is smoother than oral breathing. By doing this, you are exercising your diaphragm muscle. You will feel your chest enlarge, your back will straighten, and your elbows will rise on your chest. When your chest feels full of air, pause lightly for a moment or so.

Exhalation Exhale passively. Your lungs will expel the air without extra effort.

Forced Exhalation When you feel that there is still some air in your lungs, exhale in a series of bursts, until you feel that there is no more air in your lungs. Exhaling should be done slowly, and with a controlled intensity. Puff as if you were blowing on a candle flame, but did not want to blow it out.

During this exercise, you will feel that your sides have contracted, that your elbows are very relaxed, and that your chest has risen slightly. Sometimes, people experience a small cramp in their stomach muscles, which simply means that their abdominal muscles are working.

You will be well aware of movements of your baby during this exercise. The goal of this exercise is to learn the different stages of breathing and to strengthen your muscles, particularly the diaphragm muscle. (The name given to this type of exercise is diaphragmatic breathing.) This is the first exercise that you will practice during your course. You can practice while lying on your side or back. Practice the exercise in two series of four or five times a day.

Second Type of Breathing

The second type of breathing is a type of panting. There is no forced exhalation during this exercise. Breathing is not deep and long, but it is superficial and fast. You should inhale and exhale rapidly and rhythmically (two times a second).

In this way the diaphragm is held in balance and does not push on the uterus. Begin your exercises with the deep breathing, then practice panting. Try to pant rhythmically for long periods of time. Begin with a 15-minute practice, then extend your time. If you can, pant for 45 minutes. To restore normal breathing, take a very deep breath and exhale slowly. These exercises tend to dry out the throat, so don't be alarmed if this happens.

The first exercise can be done at all stages of labor. The second is reserved for long, painful contractions. The second type is more tiring than the first.

Neuromuscular Relaxation

Controlling the nervous system during labor is very important. As we have mentioned, training the nervous system to deal with pain is central to controlling it. Muscle control contributes greatly to reeducating the nervous system. A learned response will govern the natural defensive response to pain. Controlling the reactions of certain muscles of the body to pain is a path to the brain's pain response. We have discussed controlling the diaphragm and abdominal muscles. Now let us focus on some other muscles.

Controlling the facial muscles (this includes the speech muscles, the tongue, chewing muscles, and muscles of expression) and the muscles of the hands (particularly the fingers) is a way of controlling the brain's pain response. Even though these muscles form a small percentage of the body's total muscle mass, their control takes up a comparatively large area of the brain. By controlling them, a large area of the brain is controlled.

The other advantage of this type of muscle control is the conservation of oxygen. The natural defensive reactions (agitation, stiffening up, irregular breathing) use up oxygen that is needed for the uterine area and by the child. If the uterus does not get enough blood and oxygen, it tires, and contractions become more painful. The pain cycle then begins.

Relaxing the muscular response to pain is not easy. Most people start out stiffly, not ever having had a need to control pain. Through careful, patient training, you will be able to acquire this skill. In this way you will control pain; it will not be controlling you.

To relax the different muscles, you must first learn where they are. Begin by trying to control your arm muscles. Extend your right arm. As you do this, try to become aware of the extensor muscles. These muscles are responsible for making your arm straight and stiff. Now, let your arm fall. In the beginning, this will be difficult. You will probably try to control the fall of your arm. To find out if you are able to relax your arm, hold your arm out. Have your husband or a friend support your arm, relax the arm, and then have the other person quickly withdraw the support. You may be surprised to see your arm stay straight. This means that your arm is tense. If the arm falls, you have succeeded in relaxing the muscles. After you have learned to control the muscles in your right arm, try the same thing with your left arm. Gradually, your brain will learn what you want it to do and give the correct instructions. These exercises can be applied to any part of the body. After you have learned to control your arm muscles, try to control the other areas of your body.

Lying on your back, alternate between the two sides of your body. Prop your knees and head with pillows, and exercise your arms.

Relax all your muscles for two minutes. Have your partner verify that you are relaxed. Have your partner shake your forearm lightly. If your hand moves gently, you are relaxed. If you are not relaxed, your hand will be stiff.

Repeat this with different groups of muscles, legs and arms, alternately or together.

Your face should also be relaxed. Close your eyes, and relax the muscles of your face. You will feel these muscles relaxing. When the mouth opens slightly, you know that you are relaxed, because the maxillary muscle is not tense.

You must also learn to control the muscles of the perineum, the area between the vagina and the anus. To do this, you must become aware of them. Imagine that you need to urinate but that you must contain yourself for a few minutes. These are the muscles that you must control. Control of the perineum is very important at the moment of expulsion. All the other muscles will be tense in the effort to deliver the baby. If you can keep the perineum supple, the baby will pass out of the lower pelvis more easily. Your instructors will help you with any problems you are having.

3

In discussing abnormal pregnancies, many frightening terms may be mentioned. We would like to define them and inform you of some common problems.

MISCARRIAGE

Expulsions of the fetus before the 180th day are called miscarriages. After the 180th day expulsions of the fetus are called premature deliveries.

Causes of miscarriage are numerous. Some common ones are:

A serious illness in the mother (typhoid, scarlet fever, diabetes, etc.).

Use of alcohol and tobacco heightens chances of miscarriage.

Uterine malformations, uterine infections, and abnormalities of the cervix.

Hormonal imbalances from either the mother or the placenta.

Abnormal chromosomal developments that don't allow the fetus to grow properly.

Often, there is no apparent reason for a miscarriage. Sometimes a woman will have a miscarriage during her first pregnancy and have none thereafter. On the other hand, if a woman suffers from repeated miscarriages, a complete examination is necessary.

Problems in the Development of a Pregnancy

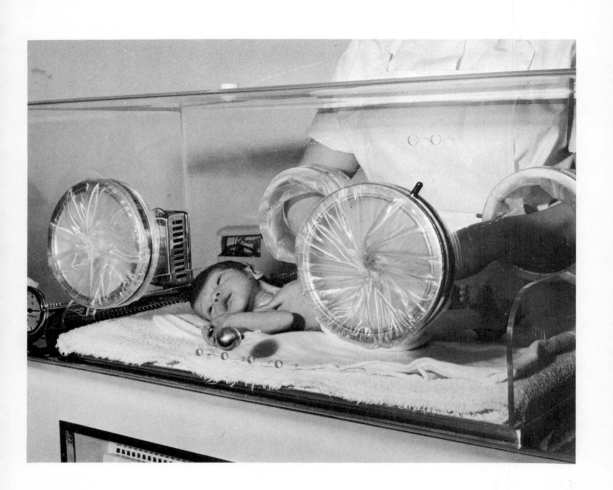

Miscarriages occur in three phases:

Threatened miscarriage
Inevitable miscarriage
Actual miscarriage

A threatened miscarriage is usually accompanied by two signals: (1) a flow of dark blood, irregular in quantity and appearance,
and (2) pain in the uterine area, which is due to contractions. Some
women notice pain in the kidneys.

These signals can be very slight, but this does not mean that
they are not serious. If a pregnant woman notices any blood, she
must consult her doctor immediately, even though some bleeding
occurs in 30 percent of all pregnant females. She should stop all
activity, rest, and refrain from sexual relations until she sees her
doctor.

The doctor will check to see if the cervix is still closed. If it is
still closed, a miscarriage may be avoided. The doctor may find a
malformed uterus or a fibroid tumor. Often, nothing abnormal is
found, but certain precautions must be observed. Check with your
doctor if you have any questions about what you should or should
not do. Each case will have to be considered individually, but the
pregnancy will probably continue without further problems, and a
healthy child will be born.

If these precautions do not help, the outcome may not be as
good. The following symptoms indicate a worsening of the situation:

Pain in the abdomen increases, and bleeding continues. Laborlike
contractions take place.

Signs of a developing pregnancy stop. The woman does not continue
to gain weight, and signs of fetal movement lessen. Negative pregnancy test results show that the pregnancy has been interrupted.

If these events take place, a miscarriage will inevitably follow
in a few days or weeks. The second stage of miscarriage, inevitable
miscarriage, has been entered. Contractions become stronger, and
more and more blood is passed. If you cannot get in touch with
your doctor, admit yourself to the hospital. Keep everything that has
been passed for future analysis. Once the embryo has been passed,
bleeding usually stops. The age of the egg is often an indication of
why the miscarriage occurred.

If the miscarriage occurs during the second or third month, the egg is rejected in two stages, corresponding to hormonal insufficiencies. The miscarriage is delayed, and a minor labor takes place. Usually, it happens quickly, and with little pain. A dilation and curettage is often performed after a miscarriage.

TUBAL PREGNANCY

A tubal pregnancy occurs when the fertilized egg attaches itself to the wall of the Fallopian tube instead of the uterine wall. When the egg grows beyond the diameter of the Fallopian tube, the tube splits, and hemorrhaging in the abdominal cavity starts. The woman feels a sharp pain and will probably pass some blood vaginally. The pain will increase, and the woman may faint or go into shock. This is an extremely critical situation, and immediate hospitalization is required. If there is any doubt that a tubal pregnancy is the cause of

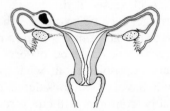

Tubal pregnancy

the pain, the patient will be examined with a laparoscope. With the laparoscope, the doctor examines the Fallopian tube. The laparoscope is inserted through an incision above the navel. If the Fallopian tube is dilated and the abdomen has blood clots in it, a tubal rupture has occurred. Immediate surgical removal of the egg and a section of the tube is necessary. If a tubal pregnancy is not found, a small surgical clip will close the incision made for the laparoscope. A short hospital stay will probably be necessary.

In some cases, the egg does not develop in the tube but alongside of it. This is called an abdominal pregnancy and is a very rare occurrence.

INTERSTITIAL (CORNUAL) PREGNANCY

A very rare occurrence, an interstitial, or cornual, pregnancy occurs when the fertilized egg attaches itself to the part of the Fallopian tube that connects to the wall of the uterus. Symptoms may resemble those of a tubal pregnancy, in which case hospitalization is vital.

HYDATIDIFORM MOLE

Hydatidiform mole is an abnormal pregnancy in which there is no embryo. The placental structure is abnormal. The villi form cysts that resemble grapes with blood clots. The grapelike formations are clear. This abnormality is marked by irregular, spontaneous bleeding, excessive vomiting, and albumin in the urine. Eclampsia, or convulsions, may also occur. The uterus expands faster than in normal pregnancy. For example, a woman may look like she is five months pregnant, and actually be only in her second month. Hormonal flow is above normal. By the fourth or fifth month the abnormal structure will be passed. Often this is accompanied by heavy bleeding. Strict observation must follow this complication to prevent infection and watch for the development of malignancies.

TOXEMIA

Toxemia may develop during the last three months of pregnancy and is marked by three findings:

Albumin in the urine.
Edema or excessive fluid retention. Weight gain is excessive, extremities become swollen, and the face is bloated.
High blood pressure.

By looking for these signs during prenatal visits, toxemia can be prevented. If it is not treated, serious consequences may result for both the mother (eclampsia, detachment of the placenta) and the fetus (death).

Because of modern prenatal care, eclampsia is very rare. Eclampsia results from the edema of the cervix. Episodes of violent headaches and a feeling of suffocation (lasting about 2 minutes) are followed by a longer coma. The episodes can repeat themselves. Often these episodes start the labor process, and the child will be born either emaciated or dead. Sometimes a cesarean delivery is necessary.

PLACENTA PREVIA

Placenta previa happens when the placenta is attached to the lower section of the uterus. It shows up during the last 3 months of pregnancy. The major symptom is bleeding with pain almost never pres-

Normally attached placenta   Marginal placenta previa   Total placenta previa

ent. Hospitalization is urgent. A surgical staff should be available, because it is impossible to predict the outcome of the bleeding. Often, resting will halt the bleeding, and the pregnancy will continue normally to term. Sometimes the bleeding will continue, and transfusions will become necessary. If the placenta is attached centrally, a cesarean delivery will be necessary.

HYDRAMNIOS

With hydramnios, the uterus contains more amniotic fluid than normal (a normal amount is about 1 pint). A woman with hydramnios may have 3 or 4 pints. This may happen in cases of jaundice or diabetes or in fetal illnesses. Delivery is often premature.

GERMAN MEASLES

For a long time German measles was considered a minor illness, until an Australian ophthalmologist established a correlation between eye and heart malformations in newborns and the appearance of German measles during pregnancy.

German measles is a viral illness. As with all other viruses (such as chickenpox or other forms of measles), the disease can only be caught through *direct* contact with a person who has the illness; it cannot be transmitted through an intermediary person. The contagious phase begins 8 days before the skin breaks out and ends 8 days after the skin clears up. Generally, there are 16 days of incubation during which there is no sign of disease.

The first visible sign of the illness is a fever, accompanied by watery eyes, nasal discharge, and cough. Then the skin breaks out in small, reddish spots varying in size and appearance. The spots begin on the face, then spread to the rest of the body. Examination of people with the disease reveals a number of nerve groupings that are slightly swollen but not painful. The throat and roof of the mouth are red, and fever, cough, and nasal discharge continue until the rash covers the rest of the body. When the rash is gone, the person is permanently immune to the illness.

Sometimes German measles takes on different forms. In some cases no rash is present. It can also pass for a flu. In adults it can come and go without any sign of illness. The adult still develops an immunity, and the same dangers are still present for the fetus. The percentage of adult women who have had German measles before reaching the age of 20 varies from place to place.

Consequences to the Fetus

The amount of danger posed to the fetus through exposure to German measles depends on when the fetus is exposed. The first trimester is the most vulnerable time, but the risk continues throughout pregnancy. What exactly are the risks?

Out of 100 women who have German measles during the first trimester, 14 to 20 spontaneous abortions will take place.

7 to 8 infants will be born dead.

Between 20 and 40 infants will be born with the following malformations, listed in order of frequency: heart defects (arterial canal, interarticular or interventricular communication), eye defects (cataracts, microphthalmia, retinitis pigmentosa), and malfunctions of the internal ear and the nervous system.

Treatment and Prevention

What should you do if you have been exposed to rubella and are not sure if you are immune? Contact your doctor *immediately*. If possible, he or she will confirm whether the person that you have had contact with has German measles.

You can be tested to see if you are immune to German measles as a result of having had it previously. If the test is positive, you are immune, and the fetus is also protected. Another test is required 15 days later to verify that the first test did not show immunity resulting from German measles that were already in progress.

If the test is negative, you are vulnerable to rubella, but you don't necessarily have it; 15 to 20 days later you should have a second test. If the second test is negative, you have not contracted rubella. If the second test is positive, you have been infected with German measles. Your doctor will help you decide whether the pregnancy should be continued.

Of course, vaccination of all children, especially young girls before puberty, will eliminate the possibility of pregnancy with German measles. (Exposure during childhood to other children with the disease also strengthens immunity.) In some states children cannot be enrolled in school without such vaccinations. All women who are not immune should be vaccinated on condition that they do not become pregnant during the 3 months following the vaccination.

TOXOPLASMOSIS

Toxoplasmosis results from a parasite. It is very widespread and usually not serious. However, it can cause disorders in the fetus if the mother contracts the disease while pregnant. Possibilities for discovery and prevention merit more concern than is ordinarily given to the subject.

The toxoplasmosis parasite exists in meats and vegetables and in vaginal inflammations. The reproductive cycle of this parasite has been well known since 1970.

In nature the principal element in this reproductive cycle is found in cat excrement. The parasite is dropped onto the ground, where it can enter plant life. Other animals can then ingest the parasite. Human infection can take place through direct contact with dirt on which cats have excreted, through the eating of raw vegetables that have grown in earth on which cats have excreted, or through animal meat that is not well cooked.

Toxoplasmosis affects adults in the same manner as infants. The lymph nodes swell up. This is particularly true of the glands under the chin. After the disease runs it course, the person is immune to any further infection. The disease is not serious in the vast majority of cases, although, very rarely, grave complications do arise. Fever, flulike symptoms, aching in the joints, or a rash can also develop.

Since an immunity results from having had it, it is good for young girls to contract it to protect their future pregnancies. If they have the immunity, all future contacts with the parasite will be without consequence. If the mother has never had the infection, the fetus will contract it from her if she is exposed.

It is possible to find out if a person has had the disease through a blood test called the Sabin dye test. The blood is diluted and mixed with live toxoplasmas. If the person being tested is immune, the antibodies in the blood will destroy the toxoplasmas. If the person has never had the disease, the toxoplasmas are not affected by the blood.

In which cases is the fetus affected? As we have said, contamination of the fetus occurs when the mother contracts the disease while pregnant. The parasite goes throughout her system and reaches the fetus through the placenta barrier. To reach the fetus, the toxoplasma must develop for 2 or 3 months in the placenta. This leaves doctors enough time to protect the fetus if the disease is discovered quickly. If the infection takes place before conception, the fetus will not be affected by it. If infection takes place during the first month, miscarriage becomes a probable consequence. However, if contamination does occur, the mother and the doctor may consider aborting the fetus because of the complications that can develop. If the infection takes place during the second trimester, serious complications can also occur. During the third trimester, the fetus simply experiences a mild and latent form of the disease, and no damage occurs.

In four-fifths of the cases of congenital toxoplasmosis, no apparent abnormality results. Discovery occurs at birth and allows doctors to avoid any further complications resulting from the disease. In one fifth of the cases, observable abnormalities develop. They can affect the nervous system, the eyes (chorioretinitis, or inflammation of the retina; or microphthalmia, abnormally small eyes), or the liver (neonatal jaundice).

How can a pregnant woman protect herself from this disease? First of all, women should have blood tests to find out if they have ever had the disease. They should have the test before they become pregnant. Any women who are pregnant and who show a negative test result (meaning that they are susceptible to the disease) should observe the following precautions:

Avoid eating raw vegetables that have grown in earth on which cats have excreted and meat that is not well cooked.

Observe basic hygienic measures. Wash hands carefully after handling any dirt.

Avoid all contact with cats.

Be tested every 6 weeks so that treatment can be given should the disease be contracted.

AMNIOCENTESIS

Amniocentesis is a method of finding out information about the fetus by examining the amniotic fluid that surrounds it. This fluid contains cells that originate from the fetus. By studying them, one can discover important physical and chemical facts about the developing fetus. The fluid is often withdrawn during the sixteenth week (during which time the flow of antibodies increases) to test genetic characteristics. Metabolic problems and the Rh factor can also be diagnosed by studying the chromosomal makeup of the cells. In this way, abnormalities in the fetus can be detected and treated early. Sex-linked abnormalities and the sex of the child can be discovered using this method. Amniocentesis is also used to diagnose fetal illnesses or to find out why a pregnancy has passed the term of delivery.

The test cannot be performed before the fourteenth week without endangering the life of the fetus. Before the fourteenth week there is not enough fluid to take a sample without risk to the fetus. Any cultures that have to be made from the cells take about a month to develop. Extremely specialized laboratories are required to perform the tests.

SUTURING THE CERVIX

If a woman has had a miscarriage previously because of an incompetent cervix, sutures can be placed in the cervix to strengthen it. This is done in the early stages of pregnancy, before the fourth month. This enables many women to carry their pregnancies to term, but it does not work in all instances. The stitches can easily be removed before labor begins.

THE PREMATURE BABY

Theoretically, one should only use the term *premature* for babies born before the end of the thirty-seventh week. For reasons of practicality, however, the term is more broadly applied to all babies of *low birth weight* (2500 grams—5 pounds, 7.5 ounces—or less).

Low birth weight can result from a number of circumstances.

Some are full-term babies who did not achieve normal weight. This can happen for no apparent reason. These babies are called hypotrophic. Others are born with a low birth weight resulting from a problem pregnancy. Others are born before the thirty-seventh week and are truly premature.

There are a variety of causes of prematurity. Twins are sometimes born before the pregnancy reaches term. Pregnancies marked by passage of blood (due to hormonal imbalance or uterine infection), toxemia, uterine abnormalities (preceding problems with spontaneous abortion), or an abnormal placenta (placenta previa) can result in low birth weights. External factors can bring on a premature delivery, also. Trauma resulting from an accident, a fall, or sickness (hepatitis or influenza and, less commonly, tuberculosis, diabetes, or toxoplasmosis) is sometimes the culprit. Low-income groups also have a higher incidence of prematurity.

The appearance of the premature child differs from that of the full-term baby. He or she is smaller (around 18 inches, perhaps less), but more noticeable is the emaciated look that the child has. Full-term babies are usually rounded out and may even be plump looking. The premature baby has not yet put on weight; the skeleton is more prominent, and the skin may sag in places. The face is thin, but the features are fine and distinct. The muscles are flabby and underdeveloped. The skin is covered with lanugo, a fine, downy hair, particularly on the forehead and sides of the face, and it is ruddy. Hair is abundant. The attitude of the premature infant is different from that of the full-term baby. The arms and legs of the full-term baby are bent more because of greater muscle tension. The premature infant lies flat, and the extremities are often limp. There is less movement of the limbs than in a full-term baby. Premature infants also do not breathe as deeply as do mature infants. Adaptation to life outside the womb is much slower, depending on the duration of the pregnancy. Sucking and swallowing reflexes may be absent, and feeding must then be done through tubes. Because of underdeveloped lungs, additional oxygen is often necessary. Defenses against infection are also low, and the premature infant is less able to deal with germs. Maintaining body temperature is also difficult. More calories are burned as a result, and this, coupled with an inability to eat properly, adds up to a small reserve for the child to fall back on.

All these conditions (which vary from case to case) usually mean that the child must be put into an incubator. The conditions of life can be more closely regulated, and the child can be protected from infection. Temperature can also be regulated. Premature babies are often transferred to a specialized intensive-care nursery, and a nurse who is experienced in caring for these infants takes care of feeding, weighing, and medical needs. Mother's milk is the preferred food for premature babies. It can be given to the infant by bottle or through a tube. When the child's condition has stabilized, a formula milk can be substituted for mother's milk.

The survival of these babies depends on many factors. Weight and duration of the pregnancy are obviously important. The quality of medical care received also plays a crucial role. Mortality rises from 10 to 56% when birth weight drops from 5 pounds to 2½ pounds. The lower limit of viability is about 2 pounds. Statistics reveal that about 88% of premature babies achieve normal intellectual development, and about 84% develop normally physically.

The child is usually below normal for the first two years, but is up to normal levels of growth by the fifth year. Experience shows that these children have a more difficult time growing up than full-term babies do. Sleep and appetite may be erratic. Many problems do not stem from the fact that the child is premature but from the attitudes of the family. Anxiety exists from birth on, and often becomes a permanent fear that surrounds the child's existence and development. Many of the normal things that happen to young children (sickness, falls, assorted accidents) become major incidents and are blown out of proportion. Overprotectiveness often has a detrimental effect on the child's life.

Hospitalization of the child at the beginning of life alters the mother-child relationship. The mother may subconsciously feel cheated, because she expected to present her family with a healthy, full-term child. It is necessary to resolve these attitudes and to try to give the child as normal a life as possible. Don't let the attitudes surrounding the child become more of a handicap than the original prematurity. In this way, a "premature personality" will not develop.

Regulation of Body Temperature

Human beings are warm-blooded animals. This means that their temperature remains constant regardless of the temperature surrounding their bodies. Some animals, such as birds, are cold blooded. Their body temperature changes with the temperature of the environment.

The premature infant is somewhere in between these categories because he or she lacks the means to control body temperature. Body temperature is normally regulated through two means:

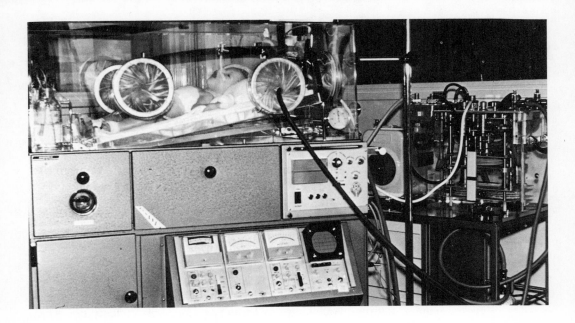

Body temperature is raised by the burning of fats. Fats are found between muscle layers. Muscle activity burns these fats and releases energy in the form of heat. Body temperature then goes up.

Evaporation lowers body temperature. Perspiration and respiration are important ways of allowing the body to evaporate fluids. Calories are also burned in these processes.

Newborns and premature infants have small amounts of muscle tissue. This limits their ability to burn fats and raise their body temperature. If exposed to the cold, their body temperatures quickly drop below normal. On the other hand, their ability to evaporate fluids is limited to respiration, since they are unable to perspire. In an overheated area, their body temperatures rise above normal.

For these reasons, newborns are usually placed in incubators. Temperature, humidity, and oxygen can be closely monitored. The environment is also germ free. Anything that must be done for the child can be done through sealed openings on the side of the incubator. Feeding and changing of diapers can be taken care of without removing the baby from the incubator. A scale can be incorporated into the incubator to avoid moving the child out of this environment for weighing.

LATE-TERM DELIVERIES

When a pregnancy lasts longer than 280 days it is a late-term delivery. A prolonged pregnancy is very dangerous for the fetus, because the placenta loses its ability to filter out germs and to deliver oxygen to the fetus. It is not unusual for pregnancies to be 8 or 10 days late. In these cases there is no cause for alarm. If the pregnancy is later than this, the doctor may want to conduct some tests, particularly if the fetus seems less active.

The doctor may perform one or more amniocentesis tests to check the color of the amniotic fluid. Vaginal discharge may also be examined. If a late-term delivery (post datism) is confirmed, labor will be induced or delivery accomplished by cesarean section.

The postmature newborn may be dehydrated and have wrinkled skin; most often, the child is normal and healthy.

CONCEPTION AND DELIVERY OF TWINS

Twins are a fairly rare occurrence, taking place in about 10 out of 1000 births. If twins have been born in either your or your husband's family, you have a greater chance of conceiving them. Twinning seems to be a recessive trait.

Finding out that twins have been conceived is always a shock. Some couples are dismayed by the financial problems and the future workload. Others view it more optimistically, thinking that raising two children together is easier than raising them separately. If you find that you are carrying twins, you must double your purchases.

There are two different types of twins. Fraternal twins represent 75% of the twins born. Two separate eggs and spermatozoa have united. Two placentas and amniotic sacs are formed. The fertilizations can result from one sexual encounter or from two closely timed ones. Both happen during the same menstrual cycle. The children are genetically different and can be of different sexes. They may not resemble each other. They can even have different fathers. Fraternal twins are most common among women who have already had children.

Placenta   Uterine sac   Amnion   Enclosing membranes
(chorion)

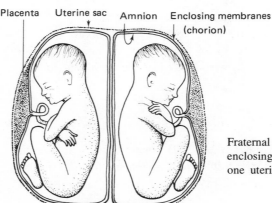

Fraternal twins. Two placentas, two enclosing membranes, two amnions, but one uterine sac.

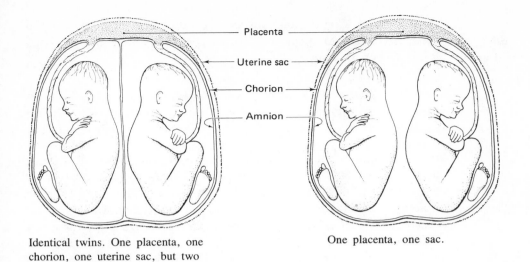

Placenta

Uterine sac

Chorion

Amnion

Identical twins. One placenta, one chorion, one uterine sac, but two amnions.

One placenta, one sac.

Identical twins come from one fertilized egg. They resemble each other very closely. They are genetically the same. Intellectually they are the same; their temperaments are often similar, and any inherited disorders are the same.

Identical twins can be formed at two points in embryonic development. A division can occur after the first cell division. Two placentas and amniotic sacs develop. In these cases it is possible to confuse fraternal and identical twins. Microscopic examination of the placentae reveals what kind of twins have been born.

More often, the division occurs at the embryonic knob stage. In these cases, two amniotic sacs develop, but there is only one placenta. In rare cases, the division takes place after the embryonic knob stage, and Siamese twins are born. With identical twins, one can be much larger than the other because of the shared placenta.

The pregnancy develops normally, and sometimes no one thinks of the possibility of twins. Fatigue and vomiting may be more marked. The volume of the uterus is larger than normal. Prenatal care must be more thorough than normal because hypertension, edema, and loss of albumin happen more easily than in a normal pregnancy. Frequent analysis of the urine is necessary. Particular attention must be paid to diet, and care must be taken not to become overly fatigued.

Twins are often born prematurely. Usually, the labor is fairly simple because of low birth weights. The first delivery takes place, and a clamp is placed on the cord. Of the two, this child will be the oldest. Between contractions, the doctor verifies the position of the second child. Contractions reappear about 20 minutes later. It is often necessary to break the second bag of water. The delivery follows soon thereafter.

MULTIPLE BIRTHS

Everyone has heard of triplets, quadruplets, and quintuplets being born, because multiple births are well publicized. Statistically, we found that out of 42 million births, 5364 were triplets, and 67 were quadruplets. That is to say that one set of triplets was born for every 7500 births, and one set of quadruplets was born for every 600,000 births.

In these pregnancies, there are often combinations of identical twins and fraternal twins. In triplets one can find three identical triplets, two identical twins and one fraternal twin, or three fraternal twins. These three categories occur equally.

As with twins, multiple births often take place prematurely. Birth weights are even lower than with twins. By the sixth month the uterus is very large. As with all multiple pregnancies, rest is crucial.

In cases of quadruplets, quintuplets, or sextuplets, the mortality rate is very high because of extremely low birth weights. Survivors have a difficult time until they mature. Multiple births have become more common because of the use of fertility drugs. Of 78 pregnancies resulting from fertility drugs, 47 resulted in one birth, 5 in triplets, 2 in quadruplets, and 1 in sextuplets.

4

In the time before the baby is born, you will probably want to assemble a good part of the necessary wardrobe. Your mother and close friends will undoubtedly offer you advice on what to buy. Many considerations will affect your final decisions. Should you buy easy-care synthetics or natural fibers? A lot depends on your own preferences, your lifestyle, and your budget. In this chapter we would like to offer some guidelines for your purchases.

WARDROBE FOR THE NEWBORN

Today you have at your disposal a wide range of fabrics for your child's wardrobe. You can purchase both synthetic and natural fibers or a mixture of both.

Synthetic materials are very popular. The price is often lower than that of natural fibers, and they are very easy to wash. Nonetheless, many doctors advise against them, especially if the garment will touch the baby's skin. Items in this category include sheets, hats, diapers, and sweaters.

There are several reasons why they are not recommended. Synthetic fibers are more likely to provoke an allergic reaction than natural fibers. These allergies could turn up at any time. Your child will come in contact with synthetics for his or her entire life, so it wouldn't be good to develop a sensitivity so early in life. Synthetics can also cause rashes.

Upkeep for synthetics may not be as easy as it first seems.

Preparations for the Arrival of the Baby

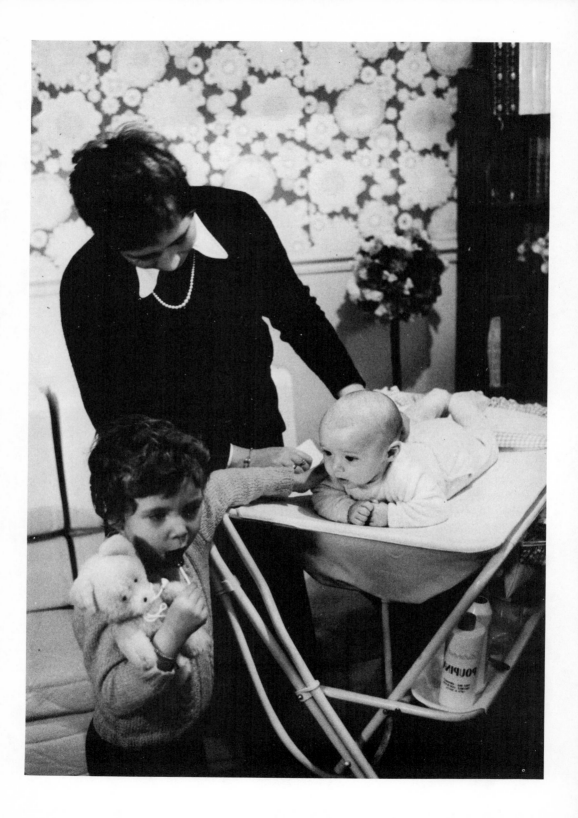

Many microorganisms and fungi circulate in our environment and may get into the fibers of our clothing. Washing in hot water destroys many of these organisms, but synthetic fibers may not be able to withstand these temperatures, and so the germs that may be in them won't be killed. Since many of these microorganisms are resistant to treatment (by antibiotics or soaps), it is better not to expose your infant to them. These microorganisms can cause rashes or infections of the mucous membranes.

Diapers

Generally, two types of diapers are available. The first is the cotton, reuseable diaper. These diapers are either large, flat pieces of cotton that can be folded any way that you like, or ones that are prefolded for your convenience. They are pinned on the baby with diaper pins and are washed when soiled. These diapers can serve other purposes besides their main function. They can be used to wipe the baby, for baths, or for burping the baby. You may find this type of diaper more practical for the newborn, because they can be folded to the size you need.

Disposable diapers have simplified the care of babies for many mothers. They come under many brand names, but generally can be divided into two types. Some are made out of cellulose and are the most popular. Others are composed of cotton padding. We do not recommend using plastic pants during the first 3 months. Use cotton pants instead. Most babies adjust well to the cellulose diapers. If any skin allergies develop, cotton diapers are suggested.

Taking care of diapers may be the most disagreeable part of having a baby. For this reason, you will undoubtedly choose the easiest method you can think of. Diaper services are widely avail-

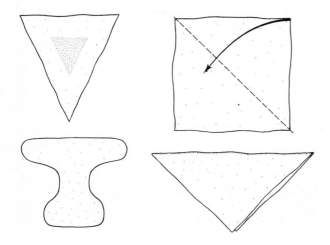

86

*Preparations
for the Arrival
of the Baby*

able. You can use them without fear, and thereby solve the entire problem.

Most people do not use a diaper service, however, and in this case you will probably use either disposable diapers or require access to a washing machine. If you are washing your diapers, you should consider the detergent that you use. Many of them are harsh, and contain a wide variety of additives. They are designed to be used for purposes other than the washing of diapers. Find a mild detergent. If you are unsure as to what brand to use, ask your doctor for a recommendation. Using too harsh a detergent can irritate your baby's skin. Rinse products and softeners, which are often marked as being beneficial to your baby's skin, are actually useless. They may even irritate the skin. We do not recommend using them.

Ways of Diapering Your Baby

If you decide to use cloth diapers, we would like to suggest a few ways of folding them. Three ways are quite popular: the triangular form, the square form, and an intermediate way that combines the triangle and the square.

First we will cover the triangular fold.

Lay the diaper on a flat surface that is clean. Fold it diagonally, as shown in Fig. 1.
Turn the triangle to the position shown in Fig. 2.
Fold the sides of the triangle toward the interior, as shown in Fig. 3.
Then fold the base of the triangle back, as shown in Fig 4.

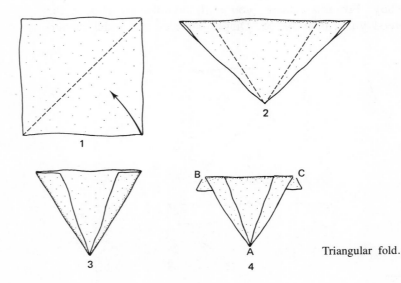

Triangular fold.

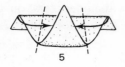

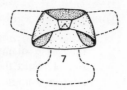

5   6   7

You now have a small triangle which you can lay the baby on. The legs go to either side of the point in front, and the side points come to the front. This is shown in Figs. 5 and 6. Pass your hand around the inside of the diaper to make sure that it fits properly. Fold the point over on itself, as shown in Fig. 7. Then pin securely. Then place a pair of cotton pants over the diaper to hold it in place. Check again to make sure that your pins are secure and closed.

Diapers can also be folded in a square form.

Lay the diaper out on a clean table, as shown in Fig. 1.

Fold the sides of the square into the diaper as shown in Fig. 2.

If you have a daughter, fold the back section down, as girls urinate toward the back section of the diaper. If you have a son, fold the front section up, as boys urinate more toward the front of the diaper. This is shown in Figs. 3 and 4.

Place the baby on the diaper. Pull the front part of the diaper through the baby's legs. About 4 inches of diaper will be in the back. Bring the corners of the back section to the front, and pin securely. This is shown in Fig. 5. Move your hand around the child's body between the diaper and skin to make sure that it is not too tight. Put on the pants when you are finished.

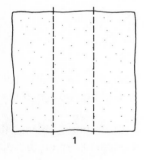

1

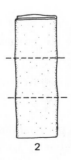

2

Girl

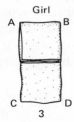

A   B

C   D

3

Boy

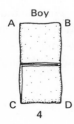

A   B

C   D

4

5

Square fold.

88

*Preparations
for the Arrival
of the Baby*

A third method of folding diapers is included for you to try. This method combines the triangular and square techniques.

Place the diaper on the table, so that the point points to you. See Fig. 1. Fold the three points into the diaper, as indicated. You will have a triangle as shown in Fig. 2.

Fold the bottom point up, to form a trapezoid, as shown in Fig. 3.

Place the baby on the diaper, and pull the lower section between the child's legs, as shown in Fig. 4.

Bring the back corners forward, exactly as for the square diaper. Pin securely, check for comfort, and put on the pants.

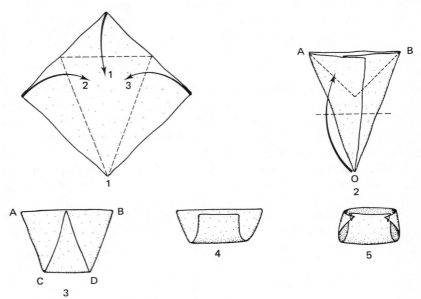

Combination of the square and triangular folds.

Nowadays, many people use prefolded diapers, in which folding is not even necessary. Time is saved, and many find that they like using them.

Plastic or cotton pants should be used with diapers. During the first three months, you may want to use cotton pants over the diapers. Cotton pants can be washed easily and can withstand higher water temperatures than plastic pants. They can also withstand more frequent launderings. Both of these factors are an advantage during the early months, because the baby must be changed very frequently. As the baby gets older, plastic pants will probably be more practical.

Clothing for Your Baby

Undershirts, along with diapers, are the base of the newborn's wardrobe. Undershirts are usually made of cotton and are worn next to the baby's skin. Usually they are white. They are adjustable to accommodate growth and usually close with snaps.

A practical garment to purchase is a variety of tee shirts. They come in a variety of fabrics. The elastic nature of the material prevents it from losing shape and allows for growth. They come in either long or short sleeves. It may be better not to put these on newborns, because they may be frightened when you pull them over the head. You can try them during the second month.

Sweaters come in a wide variety of colors and fabrics. During the winter, light wool sweaters are recommended. They can be closed in a variety of manners. Because buttons are difficult to manipulate on such small garments, snaps, zippers, and Velcro closings are more practical. Buttons down the back are not recommended because they are uncomfortable for the baby and difficult to handle. Washing wool sweaters is easy. They should be rinsed out in the sink with lukewarm water. Sweaters of other fibers may be laundered. Occasionally you may see beautiful angora sweaters for small babies. We advise against these, because the long fibers tend to get on the baby's face and in the nostrils. This also applies to synthetic fibers that are long. Upkeep for this type of garment is also very difficult.

If you don't want wool sweaters in the winter, you might consider heavier cotton shirts. They are either long or short sleeved and come in a variety of styles and colors.

Stretch suits are very practical because they completely enclose the child, keeping all the child's clothing in place. They are excellent for winter wear. Additional sweaters can be placed over the stretch suit for more warmth. The legs and feet are also well covered. Stretch suits can be substituted for a variety of garments. It is advisable to buy several of these, so they can be changed and washed frequently. The baby can also sleep in them. Stretch suits are particularly good for the first month, because they don't have to be pulled over the child's head. Most of them have a zipper down the front. Stretch leotards can add additional warmth during the winter months.

Accessories

Bibs come in a variety of shapes and sizes. For the newborn, we recommend a cotton bib. Besides being a natural fiber, it is very

90

*Preparations
for the Arrival
of the Baby*

absorbent. Later on you may want to buy plastic bibs. When purchasing bibs, look at the closing. Tie bibs are superior to snap bibs because they are more adjustable. A snap closure that is too tight for your child is uncomfortable and could cause a sore from rubbing. Be alert for any signs of sensitivity to coloring or sizing in fabrics.

Some babies scratch themselves while they are sleeping. Mittens are available that will prevent this.

Keep paper tissues on hand. They will serve you in a variety of ways.

Shoes are necessary in the winter but not in the summer months. During the summer months socks with a light elastic top are recommended. Make sure that the elastic is not too tight. Leaving the feet bare when the weather is very hot is a good idea. For the winter, find a soft shoe that can accommodate heavier socks. Many mothers use booties during the winter.

In summary, here is a list to guide you in your purchases. These are enough for one week.

24 diapers
 6 pairs of cotton pants
 6 cotton undershirts
 5 stretch suits
 6 tee shirts, sweaters, or cotton shirts
 3 bibs
 3 sets of shoes or booties
 3 pairs of socks
 3 pairs of stretch leotards
 2 or 3 sets of crib sheets and pillowcases

THE BABY'S ROOM

The arrangement of the baby's room is determined by the furniture and the space available. Outside circumstances limit you in some ways, but you should try to make the best area for the baby you can. This will cause the least disruption of your family routine.

A calm, relatively quiet area should be chosen if the baby doesn't have a separate room. The room should be well ventilated and well lighted. The temperature should be between 67 and 70 degrees. If an additional source of heat is necessary, an electric floor heater is recommended. Gas heaters should not be used. The room should not be allowed to get too warm. Older children must be told not to tamper with heaters.

If the humidity is not high enough, a vaporizer may be used. If your child has a cold or difficulty breathing, your doctor will help you decide on the level of humidity and best use of the vaporizer. Make sure that the child cannot reach any of these machines.

Arranging the baby's room should not be a difficult problem. Consider your needs, your daily routine, and what is available for your use. Choose the most practical solutions to the matter at hand.

If you cannot give the baby a separate room, you might think that sharing your own bedroom is a good solution. At first glance, it appears inviting. Your bedroom is quiet during the day and is probably one of the calmer rooms in the house. At night, though, things become more difficult. Your bedtime must fit in with the baby's schedule. The movements of the child may disturb your sleep. If possible, it might be a good idea to move the crib into an adjoining room for the night.

The Choice and Arrangement of Furniture

Simplifying your daily routine should determine the furnishings of the baby's room. Cribs come in many shapes and sizes. If the crib is washable, the daily care of your baby will be easier. It should be about waist height so you don't have to bend down too far. Cribs generally are equipped with a mattress and a flat pillow. The mattress should be covered with plastic to simplify cleaning and covered with a clean sheet. It is debatable whether the pillow is necessary. Most children sleep well without one. In any case, NEVER use an adult-sized, fluffy pillow for a baby. The child could easily suffocate in the bulk of the pillow.

Using a baby carriage for a crib is not recommended because it is very difficult to keep clean on a regular basis. Use of an adult-size bed is also a problem, because it is more difficult to change the sheets often on an adult bed.

Changing tables are higher than regular tables to aid you in changing the baby. It is a good idea to put the changing table in the bathroom or near a source of water. Keep the items that you need close to the table to avoid carrying them to the table for every change. To help prevent the baby from falling off of the table, place it next to a wall. Some changing tables have a bath attached. We have found them to be a little low and somewhat unstable.

The baby can be bathed in the sink during the first three

92
*Preparations
for the Arrival
of the Baby*

months. After this time, the baby is too large to be bathed in this manner. Also, there is a danger of banging the baby's head on the faucet. For these reasons we recommend that you purchase a light-weight, easy-to-store plastic bathtub. There is less chance that your child will be injured in a plastic tub. The tub can be placed on the changing table to make it higher. The baby is closer to you, and you don't have to bend to give the bath. You have more control of the situation.

A few items are helpful, but not indispensable. A set of shelves near the changing table might be a good idea. It is not necessary to have a scale to weigh the baby.

THE MOTHER'S WARDROBE

Don't forget to pack your suitcase for your hospital stay. Check with your hospital to see if they have a list of recommendations. Here is our list:

1 bathrobe
1 pair of slippers
3 nightgowns, 1 of which is short and full for labor
  pajamas, if you like
  toiletries

Pack your suitcase at the end of your eighth month to avoid last-minute confusion.

5

Labor and delivery are the processes through which the fetus leaves its uterine environment and begins its physical life apart from the mother. It is a bit of a struggle for both the mother and the child. During labor the infant is subject to uterine contractions for many hours. For the mother, the process involves patience, courage, and confidence. In this chapter we discuss the major aspects of labor because the more you know about what is occurring, the better participant you will be.

Childbirth happens in two stages. The stage from the onset of contractions to before the birth is called labor. The stage following labor, in which the child emerges from the womb, is called delivery.

Nature has given both mother and child a few structural advantages to make labor and delivery easier. Special muscles stretch the perineum to allow the baby's head to pass. The entire lower pelvic area retains fluid to cushion the movements of the bones and to make muscles more elastic. The bones of the baby's head have not joined together yet, which makes the head somewhat compressible as it passes through the pelvis.

THE PROGRESSION OF LABOR

During pregnancy the uterine structure has been modified in preparation for labor. By the end of pregnancy the uterus can be divided into three sections: the body, the lower section, and the neck, or cervical canal. Before pregnancy the uterus weighs about ½ pound. It weighs about 3½ pounds by the end because of an increase in

Labor
and Delivery

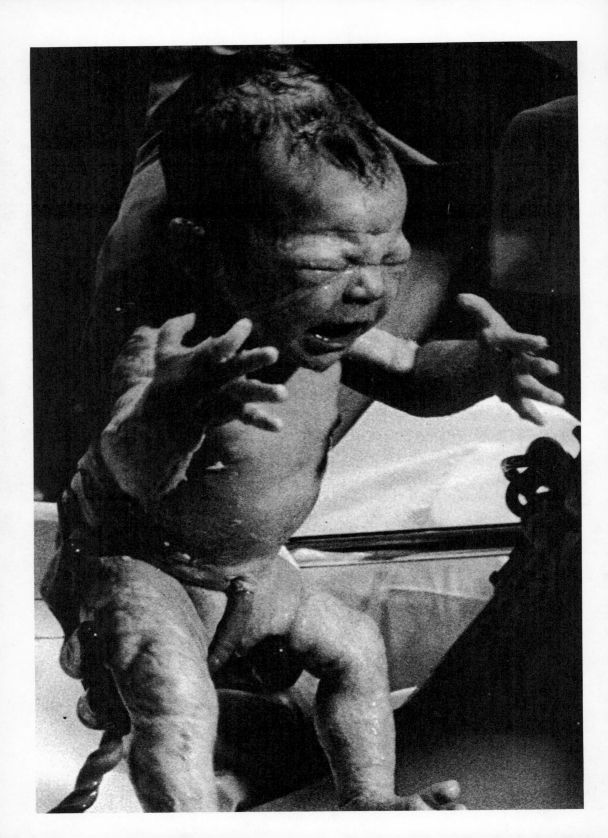

number and size of muscle tissues. Because of the extra fluid retained by the body, the muscle fibers glide back and forth over one another. The uterus remains sufficiently thick to hold the fetus while still being elastic. The lower section, which holds the baby's head before delivery, is thinner than the body of the uterus. The cervical canal or neck is quite soft and closes the base of the uterus at the cervix, which separates the internal structures from the external ones. The neck and the cervix, which are normally only a few millimeters in diameter, must open wide enough to allow the baby to pass. Uterine contractions open up the cervix and neck so that the baby can be born.

Effacement of the Cervical Canal

Before labor begins, the neck of the uterus is still at its normal length. What effect do contractions have on this part of the uterus? As mentioned previously, the uterine muscle fibers form a spiral from top to bottom. The spiral is almost horizontal at the base and becomes more oblique toward the top. At the base the fibers resemble rings piled on top of one another and connected together in an accordion-like fashion.

During a contraction the upper fibers become almost vertical and pull up on the lower fibers inserted in the neck. As the cervical neck and cervix are opened, the neck widens until it becomes indistinguishable from the uterus itself. This is called the effacement of the cervical canal and is the first sign of labor. The mucous plug in the cervical canal is dislodged and passed at the beginning of effacement.

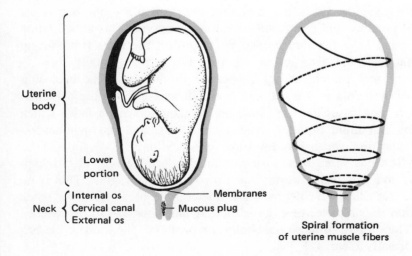

Uterine body

Lower portion

Neck { Internal os / Cervical canal / External os

Membranes — Mucous plug

Spiral formation of uterine muscle fibers

Dilation

When the cervical canal has effaced, the external orifices (cervix, vagina) are in the center of the lower section of the uterus. The tip of an index finger can be inserted into the cervix. Dilation has begun. The muscle fibers slowly pull the cervix open to a full dilation of 10 centimeters (see illustration). With full dilation the canal is large enough to let the fetus pass.

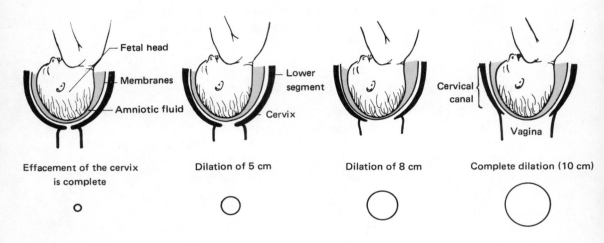

Effacement of the cervix is complete

Dilation of 5 cm

Dilation of 8 cm

Complete dilation (10 cm)

The Bag of Waters (The Amniotic Sac)

The bag of waters, composed of an outer membrane that contains the amniotic fluid, the fetus, and the placenta, rests directly on the cervix when effacement is complete. At the end of dilation the cervix has opened fully, and the bag of waters is in direct contact with the vagina. Each time a contraction takes place, the bag is put under pressure and is pressed down on the cervix. This aids dilation somewhat. The membranes and fluids protect the fetus from strong contractions and also act as a barrier for germs. Usually there is only a small amount of liquid between the head and the enclosing membrane. This is a good sign and indicates a favorable presentation. In rare cases the bag of waters contains too much fluid, which means that more liquid is between the fetus and the membranes. This may indicate a less favorable presentation.

The bag often breaks spontaneously during labor. If this happens, you will feel a warm fluid flow out of the vagina. This is no cause for alarm. Sometimes the doctor will break the bag when dilation is complete, or even earlier, if the labor has to be speeded up. The rupture of these membranes is painless. The fluid in the bag is normally clear.

Uterine Contractions

Dilation and the descent of the fetus are the result of uterine contractions. Uterine contractions are progressive and increase in intensity, duration, and frequency as labor continues. You will be able to feel the contractions quite plainly. The preparatory contractions that you experienced during pregnancy were intermittent. Labor contractions take place at regular intervals. By noting the intervals at which contractions are occurring, you can judge how quickly the labor is progressing. From the accompanying diagram you can see that contractions at the beginning of labor are less intense than those at the end. As the contraction ends, the line of the graph drops to the precontraction level. When muscles are relaxed, they are supple. The lowest level on the graph reflects this relaxation.

In rare cases, uterine contractions are not strong enough to complete labor, or there is not enough relaxation between contractions. This results in pain and is called hypertonic labor. These labors are sometimes slower and sometimes faster than usual. Extra medication is effective in these situations and brings the labor to a more normal rate.

The number of contractions varies from person to person. However, a general figure can be given. Women having their first child usually have between 150 and 200 contractions, whereas women who have already had children average about 100 contractions.

At the beginning of labor, contractions occur about every 20 minutes and last 20 to 30 seconds. At the end of labor, contractions occur about every 3 minutes and last 1 minute.

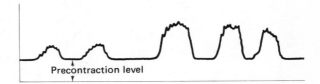

Precontraction level

Passage of the Fetus Through the Pelvis

As mentioned, the head of the child is flexed, with the chin resting on the chest. The crown of the head will be the first part to pass through the birth canal. To be born, the fetus must pass through the opening of the pelvic bones and then through the muscles of the pelvic floor.

The birth canal resembles an elbow-shaped tunnel. The larger and upper part of the "elbow" is made up of the lower uterine section and the upper section of the vagina. The lower section is made up of the pelvic floor and the pubic bones. When the widest part of the fetal head (the biparietal diameter) has passed through

97

the pelvic inlet (marked by the pubic bone in front and the end of the spine in back), engagement is said to have occurred. Successful engagement indicates that the inlet is wide enough for the baby's head to pass through, that the passage and the biparietal diameter are about the same size. In women who are having their first child, the engagement usually takes place in the last few weeks before delivery. In women who have had more than one child, engagement takes place when labor begins.

The second stage of expulsion is the descent of the head. As the descent progresses, the cervix neck bends more. The descent causes the pelvic floor to expand. The baby turns so that the head is positioned from top to bottom. This corresponds to the mother's widest dimension of the pelvic floor and vulva. The baby's head turns from the side to a more vertical position as it passes through the vagina.

THE BEGINNINGS OF LABOR

How do you know for sure that labor has begun? As mentioned, the three signs that accompany a labor that is truly underway are uterine contractions, the breaking of waters, and the passing of a mucous plug. If you are aware of them, you will not leave for the hospital too early or too late.

Uterine contractions feel somewhat sharp and are located in the upper part of the uterus. In the beginning they take place every half hour or so. The time between contractions decreases gradually from about 10 minutes in the early part of labor to as short a time as 1 minute later on. In some cases they are not as obvious as others and

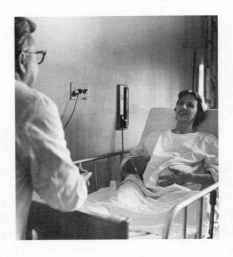

are marked only by a pulling sensation, a slight aching feeling at the base of the spinal column, or heaviness. Sensations of this type are often fleeting, but you should still keep track of when they occur. Each contraction lasts from about 30 to 90 seconds. Regular contractions mark the beginning of labor. If your contractions aren't regular, you probably aren't in labor. Continue to time the contractions. Note their frequency, rhythm, and length.

If contractions are between 3 and 5 minutes apart, you should leave for the hospital. Calmly arrange your things. If you have had other children you should leave before contractions are 5 minutes apart, as the final stage of labor can progress more rapidly with succeeding pregnancies. Make sure that there is enough time.

Perhaps your contractions will stop spontaneously. You may arrive at the hospital only to have the doctor tell you that there are no other signs of labor and that effacement has not taken place. Uterine contractions are usually regular and progressive. Do not be disconcerted if you are not in true labor. You will probably stay at the hospital for a period of time for observation. If true labor develops, you'll stay at the hospital. If not, you'll go home to await further developments.

THE DEVELOPMENT OF LABOR

Continue noting the frequency, rhythm, and duration of contractions. The hospital staff will be able to determine the progress of the labor from your data and fetal monitoring. As in most cases, the contractions will be regular, with periods of relaxation in between. The labor is developing normally.

On entering the hospital, find the most comfortable position in your bed. Many like a reclining, half-sitting position. These preliminary contractions are generally well tolerated, although some women suffer from anxiety, which makes the labor effort more difficult. Try to avoid this state of mind, because it will dissipate your energy. Remain calm. This will be easier if you have taken natural childbirth classes, because you will know what to expect. Don't think about finishing labor as quickly as possible. Don't look at your watch except to time contractions. Don't let yourself think of possible complications. Concentrate on the matter at hand.

If you are having natural childbirth, do the breathing exercises, and recall the things that you learned in class. Practice the muscle-relaxing exercises for the face and hands. Make sure that your breathing is deep and regular. Remember that both the uterus and the fetus need oxygen. Gradually, the contractions will become stronger and closer together. The people in your room should be restricted to persons who are actively involved in the labor. The person, usually your husband, who attended natural childbirth classes with you can be present to help with the breathing exercises and offer moral support.

Each hospital has different arrangements for labor, and some offer a choice of delivery techniques. You should find out what your hospital's policy is before you enter.

The nurse from the hospital will help you determine the nature of your contractions. To do this, she will place her hand on your abdomen during contractions. Frequently a fetal monitor will be used for a while, too. The nurse may suggest a different position if you find sitting difficult. She may help you with your breathing exercises during contractions or rub your back to help you relax. She'll tell you how far you have dilated and generally keep track of your progress. When you have dilated to 5 centimeters you are probably about halfway through if this is your first labor. If you have had other children, you will probably be more than halfway along. The doctor will judge how far along you are also.

The contractions will become somewhat more intense and longer. If you are having natural childbirth, during this time you will switch over to the second type of breathing. Your nurse will help you more as contractions become longer. With her hand on your abdomen, she'll tell you when to begin breathing and when to stop. You may feel warm and perspire. If your throat is dry, rinse out your mouth.

You may be instructed to switch from one type of breathing to the other. Dilation will continue, and the head of the fetus will begin to descend. The head will be resting on your perineum, and you may have the urge to begin pushing. You must not begin pushing until you are instructed to do so. If you push when the cervical canal is not completely dilated, you can irritate it and make labor more difficult. This is a very important point. Do not push until you are told to do so.

When the dilation is complete, your position will be changed, and you will be moved to the delivery room, if you are not already there. Your feet will be put in stirrups, and you may be instructed to hold on to bars on the bed when pushing. You are using the voluntary muscles of the abdomen to help the involuntary muscles push. Both muscle systems are now being used in the labor effort. As you push, the bag of waters will break, if it has not already done so. As you push, listen to the nurse. She will tell you when to push and when to breathe. The contractions may be one minute or more in duration now, and one breath will not be enough for one contraction. As you feel the need for oxygen, empty your lungs quickly, then fill them up again. Then resume pushing. Because of the effort involved, it may be necessary to breathe three or four times for each contraction.

DELIVERY

With each push, the head is moved farther along. Birth is close at hand. The vulva is now distended by the head of the child. The head crowns, then disappears back into the vagina. Several pushes later the head does not reenter the vagina, but slowly comes out, followed by the rest of the body. As you feel increased pressure on the perineum, you want to push. Don't. Instead wait for your labor

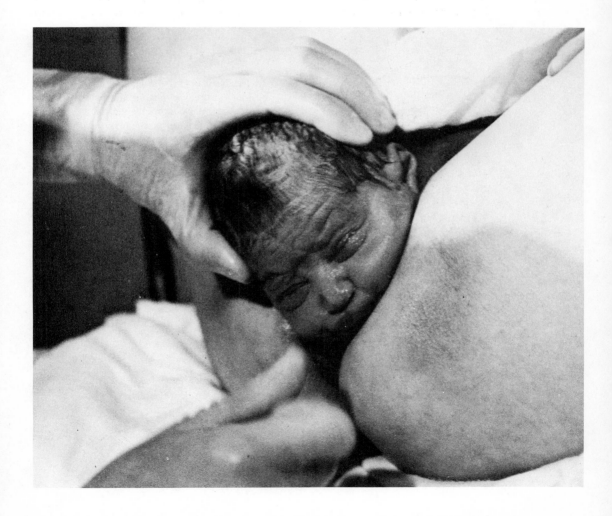

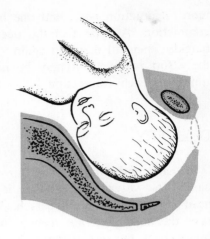

1. For engagement, the fetus bends its head (the chin rests on the chest), and the head and body are positioned obliquely in the base of the womb.

2. Here the head is engaged, and the occiput is forward and to the left. This is the most frequent and favorable position for delivery.

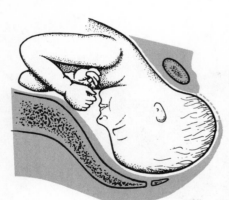

3. The head begins its descent and turns. The occiput is foremost against the pelvis, and the nape of the neck is below the pubic bone. The head begins to exert pressure on the perineum, which begins to stretch.

4. The head continues its descent. The shoulders are engaged, and the head extends beyond the pubic bone. The chin gets further and further away from the chest, and the perineum becomes distended and thinner.

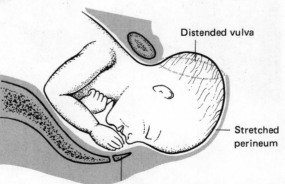

Distended vulva

Stretched perineum

The coccyx, pushed down by the head

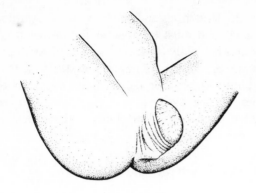

External view. One can see the shape of the head through the distended vulva.

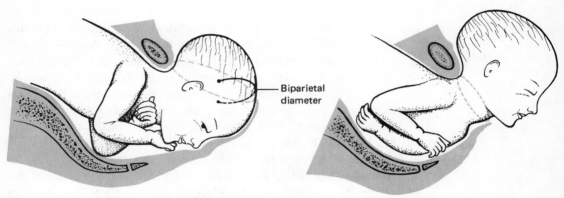

Biparietal diameter

This is the head's widest point, and the perineum is fully distended.

The head is fully out of the mother's body. The perineum has partially retracted, and the rest of the body leaves without difficulty.

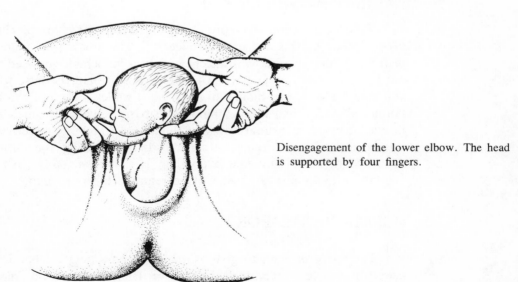

Disengagement of the lower elbow. The head is supported by four fingers.

nurse to tell you to push. Breathing and pushing are very important for you at this point, and each must be done at the proper time. Try to listen for instructions. The vulva is very distended at this point, and you need the nurse or doctor to guide the delivery to avoid damage to your own body. Slowly the baby's body comes out. First the forehead, followed by the eyes, nose, and chin. The head is now completely expelled. The rest of the body follows easily. The child is beginning a new life.

The Delivery of the Afterbirth

After the baby is born, the contents of the uterus are nearly all gone. The womb starts to contract into a mass of muscle perhaps an inch or more thick. As the uterus shrinks, the placenta separates from it and begins to slide down toward the vagina. All this usually takes a relatively short time after the baby is delivered. Some blood may be passed, but it is not a hemorrhage and should not cause you to worry. After about 20 minutes of mild contractions, the placenta is expelled. To aid expulsion, the doctor may press rhythmically on your lower abdomen. This may be unpleasant, but it is important that the placenta be expelled correctly. The uterus must be clear of all birth matter. The clear, elastic membranes will probably seem small to you. Normally, the placenta weighs about one-sixth of the baby's weight. Delivery of the placenta usually takes less than an hour.

The Uterus after Childbirth

When the uterus is empty, it contracts rapidly. This pinches off the blood vessels and controls bleeding. The area on the uterine wall where the placenta was attached is most vulnerable to bleeding but this area heals up quickly. The uterus is still hard, because it is still contracted. It will remain like this for a while as it returns to its normal size. A small flow of blood will pass. It will be somewhat heavier than the menstrual flow and should not frighten you because this is a normal occurrence. A nurse will be watching you during this time to make sure that everything is going smoothly. When everything looks normal, you will be returned to your room.

DURATION OF LABOR

It is extremely difficult to give estimates of how long a labor will take for a given individual. Length of labor depends on many factors, including the presentation of the fetus and the condition of the pelvis and surrounding tissues. Other factors aren't known until the labor is in progress. Strength of contractions varies from person to person, and changes in presentations vary. Sometimes medication and the use of instruments are necessary.

In general, though, labor lasts 8 to 12 hours for first-time mothers, with about 1 hour needed for expulsion. Women who have already had children average 3 to 6 hours for dilation and 10 to 20 minutes for expulsion.

DIFFICULTIES ENCOUNTERED IN LABOR

Sometimes difficulties are encountered during labor. Treatment is often a simple matter, followed by a return to normal labor.

Sometimes the contractions are not sufficient to open up the birth canal. If this is the case, the uterus does not relax between contractions. This causes pain to the mother, which tires her and makes her less able to respond to the situation. Uterine contractions can be made stronger and more regular by injection of oxytocin, a hormone released by the pituitary gland to cause the uterus to contract. If the uterus is not relaxing between contractions, antispasmodics can be administered. These drugs can be administered even if the abnormality is minor. The labor then can conclude normally.

Sometimes there is a problem with the descent of the head. We have mentioned that the head makes a half turn in the vagina. If this does not happen, or happens too slowly, intervention may be necessary. Forceps have a frightening reputation because they were used in times past for extremely difficult deliveries. Because cesareans are now used in difficult deliveries, forceps are no longer tools of force and are used instead for guiding or adjusting the position of the fetus. Doctors also use spatulas, which act like extensions of the doctor's hands. Another device, the vacuum extractor, attaches itself to the fetal head and helps pull the fetus out. All of these instruments can be used if the delivery must be aided.

On some women the perineum is not elastic enough to permit the head to pass without tearing. Since a clean cut heals better than a tear, the doctor cuts the perineum just before expulsion of the head. This process is called an episiotomy. It is done under local or other anesthesia and is sewn up after the delivery.

Sometimes the placenta and surrounding membranes are not expelled after delivery. In these instances the doctor removes the afterbirth.

Fetal Monitoring Equipment

Although one can listen to the fetal heartbeat with a stethoscope, many hospitals now use electronic fetal heart-rate (FHR) monitoring equipment. Fetal monitoring measures the baby's pulse during and just after each contraction of the uterus. The external monitor is attached to the abdomen of the mother and makes a graph of cardiac rhythm. The internal monitor is attached to the fetal scalp.

FHR helps medical personnel to detect, and prepare for, any unusual distress the fetus might be experiencing.

Cesarean Section

A cesarean section is the surgical removal of the fetus from the womb. Although cesareans are usually safe for mother and child, they are not performed unless they are warranted. Some difficulties that call for cesareans include a narrow pelvis, an obstructing tumor in the birth canal, or a cervix that will not dilate. If the umbilical cord has been crushed by contractions (prolapse of the cord) or if there is a poor presentation or other fetal distress, a cesarean may be used.

The incision most often used is the low transverse uterine incision. It is called the "Kerr technique." This type of incision is more likely to permit later vaginal deliveries than a vertical incision would.

Anesthesia during Childbirth

The development of natural childbirth techniques has cut down on the use of anesthesia considerably, but natural childbirth does not eliminate pain completely. As a result, each delivery situation must be assessed as it occurs. Some deliveries will require varying degrees of anesthesia.

Different types of regional anesthesia are far more common than general anesthesia. The mother remains awake during the delivery but does not feel various aspects of the labor, depending on what type of anesthesia is given. Doctors try to avoid general anesthesias and instead use more localized pain killers. This type of pain killer does not cause complications for mother or child. The labor unfolds naturally, and the mother is awake.

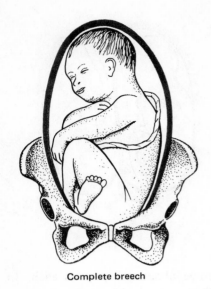

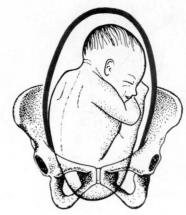

Complete breech   Frank breech

Presentations Other Than of the Head

Vertex (head) presentations are the most common and account for 95% of all deliveries. Of the remaining, 4% are breech presentations. Face presentations are rare (1 out of 250 births), as are presentations of the forehead (1 out of 1000 births). Presentations of the elbow are extremely rare.

There are three classifications of breech presentations: frank breech, complete breech, and incomplete breech. The classification depends on the position and flexion (bending) or extension (straightening) of the fetus's legs in relation to his or her buttocks.

Labor proceeds normally, but care must be taken at the delivery stage to make sure that the head follows the body quickly enough. This type of delivery is usually not a problem if the mother has had children before. Extra precautions must be observed if a woman's first labor is a breech labor. This is especially true if uterine contractions are not strong, if the woman is older, or if the child is large. In these cases, a Cesarean may be considered. Face presentations can usually be delivered vaginally, but presentations of the forehead and elbow are usually delivered by Cesarean.

In twins, the presentation is either both vertex or one breech

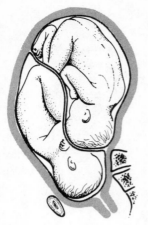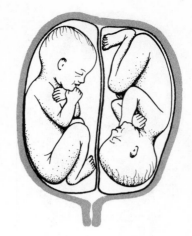

Presentation of twins.

and one vertex. Birth weights average about five pounds each. In such a case the placenta is larger than normal and is often kept for further examination in order to determine if the twins are identical or fraternal.

6

Labor is finished, and your child has cried that first cry. You know whether the baby is a boy or a girl. The cord has been cut and clamped. You want very badly to see your infant, but first the child must be cleaned carefully. The mouth, the eyes, and the nostrils must be cleaned out, and usually an antibiotic is placed in the eyes.

YOUR CHILD'S APPEARANCE

The color of your baby may be different than you have anticipated. Most often, newborns are a ruddy color. Sometimes the fingers and toes are bluish. They will turn pink in a few days. If the labor has been long, the baby may be bluish, which will disappear after a few deep breaths. Sometimes the skin has a marbled appearance. This is due to blood circulating in fine capillaries (the capillaries are red and the skin is a paler color). This is a normal appearance.

Vernix caseosa is a cream-cheese-like substance that is often found on the baby's skin. It is mainly made up of cholesterol. It serves two functions, to protect the child's skin from the amniotic fluid while in the womb and to lubricate the skin, making passage through the birth canal easier. It is reabsorbed about 48 hours after delivery. It leaves the skin very fine and velvety looking.

The amount of hair on the child's head varies from baby to baby. Hair is generally less noticeable among blonds than among brunettes.

The First Week for Mother and Child

A fine, downy hair called lanugo may cover areas of the body, especially the neck, back, and shoulders. It may also appear on the shoulders and arms. It disappears in a few weeks.

Sometimes the head is more oval than round. This shape results from pressure placed on it during delivery. A more-regular-looking shape will appear in a few days. Small yellowish dots may surround the child's mouth and nose. These dots result from sebaceous glands that have been dilated by secretions, and they disappear after a month or so.

Behavior of Your Newborn

When lying on a table, the newborn's elbows and knees are half bent, and the hands are closed. This happens because there is a tension in the arms and legs when the muscles of the spinal column are completely relaxed. This tension is a very real thing, as you discover when you try to dress the baby!

Infants usually do not move much during the hours following childbirth. When this phase has passed, some may lie quietly, crossing and uncrossing their legs as they sleep. Others are more active. They cry a lot, move their heads from right to left, and suck their fists. Already you can see the emergence of a distinct character!

The Physical Examination

Two statistics are commonly taken for newborns: weight and length. These mark the starting point for the rest of the child's development. High birth weight has traditionally been a subject of pride for mothers, so much so that it has been given a place of exaggerated importance. A newborn who weighs less than 7 pounds is as healthy as a baby with a higher birth weight. An extremely

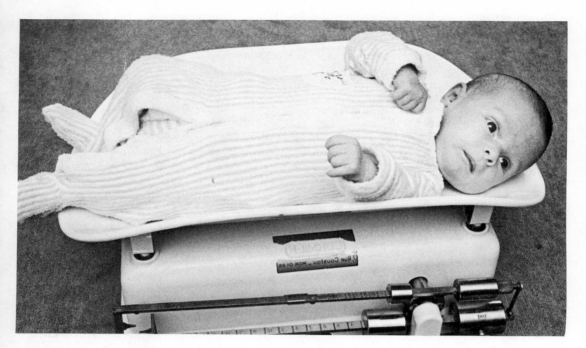

high birth weight may be a sign of an abnormal pregnancy. Apart from extremes, the middle range of development is quite broad.

Weight is one of the most important factors. It varies with the proportions of each child. Several factors are involved. The length of the pregnancy is important; obviously, a full-term baby will weigh more than a premature baby. The diet of the mother is of tremendous importance in determining birth weight. Too low a calorie intake will make the child weak and of low weight. Too much food will make the newborn unusually large (this used to be considered a favorable outcome). Ethnic and family characteristics play an important role. If the parents are big people, the child will probably inherit this trait. If they are small, the child will most likely be small.

Length of newborns depends a lot on the height of the parents. The median length is around 19½ inches. Baby boys measure between 18 and 21¼ inches, and baby girls measure between 18½ inches and 20¾ inches. Of course, individuals may vary considerably.

Respiration begins when the child cries for the first time. In crying, the lungs are filled up with air for the first time. Regular exhalation and inhalation takes place from then on, at a rate of about 40 breaths per minute.

The infant's heart beats about 120 times per minute, as opposed to 60 to 80 beats per minute for your own. The physician will listen to be sure that the beat is regular and that the frequency is normal. Respiration and heartbeat are checked soon after birth. The following items will also be checked.

The mouth, particularly the palate, will be examined to make sure that it has closed properly.

The cranium is both bony and fibrous in composition. The fontanels are the fibrous sections and form the junctions of the bony plates of the brain. The most important fontanel (the bregma or anterior fontanel) is diamond shaped and found at the top of the head. The posterior fontanel is smaller, triangular shaped, and is found in the back of the head. The measurements of these sections vary. The anterior fontanel can go almost to the top of the forehead. It is normally firm but yields slightly to finger pressure. Sometimes the fontanels are very small and seem nearly closed.

The eyes are difficult to observe soon after birth. When you catch the baby awake, you'll notice that the eyes are blue or slate

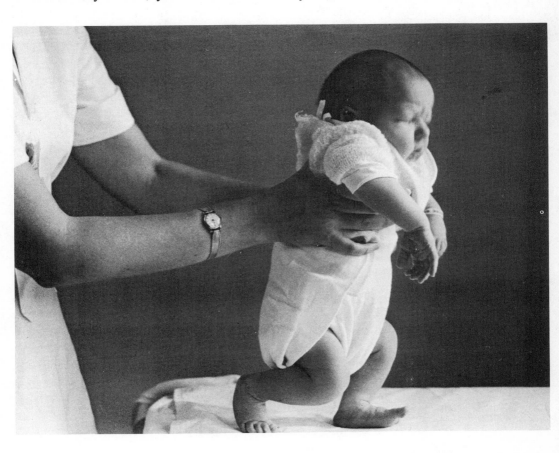

blue. If the baby has inherited brown eyes, the color will show up later. Sometimes the baby appears to squint. This is normal and will disappear as time goes on.

The spinal column is examined by running a finger down the child's back.

You may see the doctor opening and closing the child's legs a few times. This is done to make sure that the hip joints are normal and that there is no dislocation. The feet are also examined. The ankles are turned to check the mobility of the joints. The doctor also makes sure that the soles of the feet are normally oriented.

The genital organs are examined. Boys are checked to make sure that the testicles have descended, and girls are checked to make sure that the position of the urinary tract is normal.

There are several reflex actions that are normal for newborns. If the side of an infant's mouth is brushed, the baby will turn its head toward the side that was brushed. This reflex is to help the child find food and is called the rooting reflex.

When the baby is startled, two simultaneous reactions take place. The baby first throws its arms sideways, then brings them back across the body. The legs are also extended, then the knees come back to the abdomen. This is called the Moro or startle reflex.

By touching the palm of an open hand, you cause the baby to close its fingers around your finger. By touching the feet, the same reflex causes the toes to grasp. This reflex is called the Palmer grasp reflex.

If a newborn is held upright on a hard surface, with the body leaning slightly forward, he or she will take a few quick, alternating steps. This is called the step or walk-in-place reflex.

All of these reflexes indicate a normally developed nervous system. You will have the chance to observe your new child more closely. You may observe several other things.

Details of Your Newborn's Appearance

In early life, several types of marks may appear on a child's skin that do not look normal to the uninformed observer but which are not serious. We would like to alert you to them so that you won't be frightened if you see them on your child.

A child's face may be puffy during the day following delivery. This is due to water retained below the outermost layer of skin. It is often most visible on the eyelids and disappears after 24 hours.

Rose-colored patches may be present on the upper eyelids or in the center of the forehead. They are made up of groups of capillaries and are more apparent when the child cries. They disappear before 2 years of age. These patches may also be found on the nape of the neck or on the lower part of the scalp. Their contour is irregular, and the number of patches varies from child to child.

Some children have a bluish marking on the lower back or buttocks. It may be large or small and of irregular contour. These markings occur most often on children of Asian, Southern European, or African descent. They are not dangerous and disappear by 5 years of age.

Newborn rash appears quite often. It consists of reddish blotches, some of which may have white pinheads at the top. Do not squeeze them. They will disappear in a few days.

Marks of Labor on the Newborn

In addition to the things already mentioned, you may notice some of the following marks resulting from the labor. Marks of this type are often seen on the head, because the head is the focus of a lot of pressure during childbirth.

Caput succedaneum results from excessive fluid below the scalp. The fluid alters the round appearance of the skull. It is a result of pressure during dilation of the cervix, and will disappear in a few days. The fluid collects below the skin layer and does not adhere to the cranial bones. It is not painful to the child.

A cephalhematoma looks very similar but is different in important respects. It appears 2 or 3 days after delivery and has an elastic consistency. It is made up of blood that has collected under the external side of the cranial bones. This will disappear during the weeks following delivery and is not harmful.

Some children develop a subconjunctival hemorrhage in the white of the eye. It looks like a small red spot in the white and comes from a rupture of capillaries during labor. No treatment is necessary, and it, too, disappears in a few days.

If forceps were used during the delivery, red marks may be on the child's cheeks. They disappear with time.

If the child was a breech presentation, collection of blood or fluid may show up on the buttocks and external genitals. The skin is bluish and swollen. Again, this is not a serious problem, and will go away spontaneously.

THE FIRST WEEK

Until birth, the fetus lives in a liquid environment and is completely dependent on the mother for elements vital to life. When born, the baby must adapt its body to independent functioning. This requires many changes that must take place during the first few days of life.

Adaptation of the Lungs and Heart

The heart functions very differently in the fetus than in a newborn or adult. This happens because the lungs do not oxygenate the blood of the fetus. After birth, blood is oxygenated in the lungs via the circulatory system.

In the fetus the blood passes through the lungs, but the blood is not oxygenated there. This takes place in the placenta because the fetus cannot oxygenate its own blood. The cardiac chambers are connected to one another to complete the circulation of the blood. The blood passes from the right atrium to the left atrium of the heart through the foramen ovale. The foramen ovale is an opening peculiar to the fetal state.

At birth, the infant begins breathing, and the lungs become functional. When the baby cries, blood pressure increases, and more

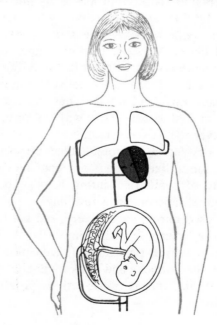

blood is supplied to the lungs. The increase of blood is then felt in the left atrium, as the blood passes through the pulmonary vein. The pressure pushes the foramen ovale against the wall of the heart, and it closes. The chambers of the heart are now independent of each other. The ductus arteriosus seals itself off, and the circulatory system has completed its adaptation from the fetal to the infant state.

The Digestive Tract

The newborn has a need to eat soon after birth. Only one food is edible at this point; this is, of course, milk. The child sucks, swallows, digests, and eliminates waste.

Sucking and swallowing instincts are well developed prior to birth. These reflexes are controlled by the central nervous system, which receives signals from the brain. A disruption of the brain functions (from prematurity, sickness, or an abnormal labor) sometimes disturbs the sucking and swallowing reflexes. In these cases a tube is placed in the infant's stomach to provide food until a suitable method of treatment can be devised.

Adaptation of the Blood

At birth, a baby has more red blood cells (between 5½ and 8 million) than a baby who is a few days old (who has around 4½ million red blood cells). The extra red blood cells are destroyed during the first day, when hemoglobin is released in the bloodstream. The hemoglobin is transformed into bilirubin, which is metabolized by the liver and eliminated by the kidneys.

In some cases the liver of the newborn is not developed enough to metabolize the bilirubin, and physiologic jaundice results. This occurs more often in premature babies than in full-term babies. It is not considered a sickness, just an adaptation to life outside the womb. The jaundice shows up between the second and fourth day. It starts slowly and increases until the color of the skin is yellow. Jaundice peaks around the seventh day and diminishes spontaneously afterward. When jaundice begins to develop, the doctor will find out whether it results from an immature liver or blood incompatibilities. Jaundice never exists at birth or during the first 24 hours after birth. During its evolution, the general health of the child is not affected. Treatment may consist of ultraviolet light and phototherapy.

Adjusting to the Severance
of Placental Hormones

While in the womb the child received hormones from the placenta. When the umbilical cord is cut, these hormones are suddenly cut off. This is the first step toward hormonal independence from the mother and forces the child to begin secreting its own hormones.

Part of the adjustment involves the time needed for the maternal hormones to leave the child's bloodstream. Until this happens, these hormones may affect the baby in several ways:

The breasts of the baby are often swollen and red. They may even secrete a few drops of milk.

The skin may develop symptoms similar to acne.

In baby boys, the testicles may become enlarged.

In baby girls the lips of the vagina may become enlarged and mucus may be secreted. Sometimes they may pass a few drops of blood.

All these occurrences are normal and vary from child to child. They disappear in a few days without treatment. It may take several weeks for the breast swelling to go down. Do not press the breasts in an attempt to drain them. Alcohol bandages are not recommended.

PERCEPTIONS OF THE NEWBORN

After having made an inventory of your child's physical traits, you may wonder what he or she is able to sense about the surroundings. Do babies see? What do they hear? We would like to give you some of the results of the many studies that have been made.

Sight

Many think that the newborn does not see. To decide if this is true, we must first define the concept of "seeing." Vision can include two different kinds of perceptions. The first is a strictly optical phenomenon. Images are caught by the eye and are transmitted to the retina. In the other sense, neurophysical considerations are involved. The stimulation of light is passed on to the brain for interpretation. A psychological process takes place in this case.

By the end of the first week, the child turns its head toward light sources. If you turn a lamp on near the baby, the size of the pupils will change. They will also dilate in darkness. This is not to say that the child can see perfect images. Studies of newborns indicate that they are slightly farsighted. Psychological integration certainly does not exist at this stage.

As mentioned, in newborns, the color of the eye is often grayish or blue and changes to a more distinct color as the weeks pass.

Taste

Proving that babies are sensitive to taste is simpler than deciding how much they can see. Taste buds are well developed when the child is born. Newborns prefer milk that is sweetened slightly to milk that is acidic in taste. This simple finding indicates that they are sensitive to taste. However, it is easy to administer a medicine that is quite bitter, so their preferences may still be forming. It is also possible that the transmission of taste perception from the tongue to the brain is slower than it will be later in development.

Smell

It is extremely difficult to collect data on this sense. Studies indicate that a sense of smell exists in some form and that babies may be sensitive to the smell of breasts and milk.

Touch

A newborn's sense of touch is different from yours. If you touch your finger to the palm, the baby will close his or her fingers around yours. Babies respond to the cold touch of the stethoscope.

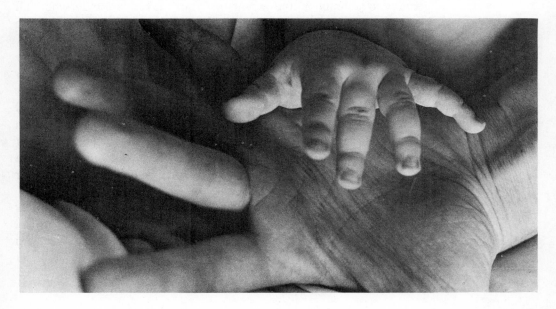

Wet diapers are not well tolerated, and touching the mouth with the breast will cause the baby's head to move toward the breast. But babies do not appear to be very sensitive to pain, and the prick of a pin does not produce immediate pain until after the seventh day. This is a controversial subject. Some doctors think that there is a delay in the complete transmission of nervous impulses.

Hearing

Although it is difficult to determine how much newborns can hear, we are certain of a few facts. Loud noises startle newborns. When you speak to them, they stop moving and listen to the sound of your voice. They learn to recognize their mother's voice, and they can differentiate varied intonations. They can distinguish between ordinary speech and cooing speech. By the first month the baby recognizes your voice but cannot differentiate your face from anyone else's.

Psychology of the Newborn

At first it may seem absurd to speak of the psychology of the newborn, but he or she does, in fact, have a world view. It is very rudimentary, but is still determined by personality and character. The world of the newborn centers on you, the mother, who is the source of everything. The newborn does not perceive itself as being separate from the mother. When leaning against you, it feels the warmth of your body. Rocking motions remind the baby of the gentle movements in the womb as you walked around, when all perceptions were softened by the thickness of the womb and the amniotic fluid.

When you hold the baby, he or she is reminded of many things that occurred before birth. The baby is accustomed to your reactions, your calm moments and your excited ones. Your arms now transmit the emotions that your entire body communicated when the baby was in the womb. Ways you were handled as an infant will be passed on to this child. The atmosphere of your home, your relationship with your husband and your attitude toward the pregnancy will all be part of the environment in which your child lives.

The way you execute your role is crucial to your child's development. Studies performed with monkeys have clearly proved this. In the first experiment, newborn monkeys were separated from their mothers and given substitute mothers. One was made of metal mesh and supplied milk. The other was made of soft fabric and did not supply milk. The majority of the baby monkeys preferred the "mother" that was soft. They lay in her arms, wasted away from lack of food, and did not go to the metal mother for milk. Apparently the need for affection is more important than the need for nourishment.

In a second experiment the baby monkeys were separated from their mothers and were placed in an environment that met their physical needs, but provided no maternal affection. When these monkeys raised their own offspring, they did so in a distant and disinterested manner.

Mothers who are overburdened with work may think that their role is being filled by an efficient performance of daily tasks. They may think that it is a waste of time to speak with the baby, who can't understand anything anyway. They rock the baby only to keep it from crying. This type of upbringing will later produce adults who cannot give affection to their own children.

Modern life makes free time a rare thing. Priorities are often placed on things as opposed to people. Our children need a balanced life. Physical needs must be met, but emotional needs should not be overlooked. Children are not able to pass on what they have never received.

KEEPING TRACK OF THE BABY'S HEALTH WHILE IN THE HOSPITAL

By noting the general appearance and reactions of the newborn, it is possible to determine accurately the child's health. Normally, he or she cries, eats, and goes back to sleep. This cycle is repeated every 3 hours if the child is getting enough to eat, and every 2 hours if he or she is not.

Weight gain or loss is a very good indication of the child's general health. It is normal for a newborn to lose from 5 to 10 percent of original birth weight during the first few days after delivery. This loss varies from child to child, with heavier children losing more than light ones. Weight stabilizes around the fifth day, and increases from then on. A lack of weight gain, or abnormally slow gain, may indicate that he or she is not getting enough to eat, or is fighting an infection. If you see any signs of infection, be sure to point them out to the doctor.

During the first day, the baby moves the bowels for the first time. The first movement consists of material in the digestive tract from the fetal state. It is tarry in texture and blackish in color. From here on, the movements will be different, depending on the type of milk that the child is drinking. If the child is breast feeding, he or she will usually have a movement after each feeding. It will be a marked yellow color, similar to scrambled eggs. This color may deepen to a greenish tone if the movement is left in the diaper for a period of time. The greenish color results from the oxidation of bile. Absorption of the liquid part of the movement by the diapers may leave it crumbly. If the child is bottle feeding, movements will be less numerous. Generally, there are one to three a day, and they are thicker and more compact.

Hygiene
for the Newborn

Hygiene is important, even during the baby's first week. Although the umbilical cord has not yet healed, you may bathe the baby. The skin is shedding the fetal coverings, and that will happen naturally.

Tap water is probably the most convenient water used to wash the child. However, you should be aware that some babies may show a reaction to chlorine and minerals in tap water. If this happens, your doctor may recommend mineral water. Soaps should not be used on the face during this time. A nonperfumed, mild soap should be used to wash the child's bottom after diaper changes. Your doctor can recommend a soap if you are not sure which brand would be best.

A good time to bathe the baby is after the second feeding of the day. Wash the face, and clean out the various folds in the skin. This includes the folds of the neck, the armpits, and thighs. Clean thoroughly (but gently) around the child's genitals and anus after each diaper change. Apply baby oil or petroleum jelly on this area to protect the skin from urine. Then put on the new diaper. The hospital will instruct you on how to care for the umbilical area, and may give you an antiseptic to make sure that no infections develop. You should clean the mouth and lips completely to make sure that no yeast infections develop. Your doctor will answer any questions that you may have on this subject. It may be necessary to remove any obstructions from the nose. Use cotton-tipped swabs for this, and proceed gently.

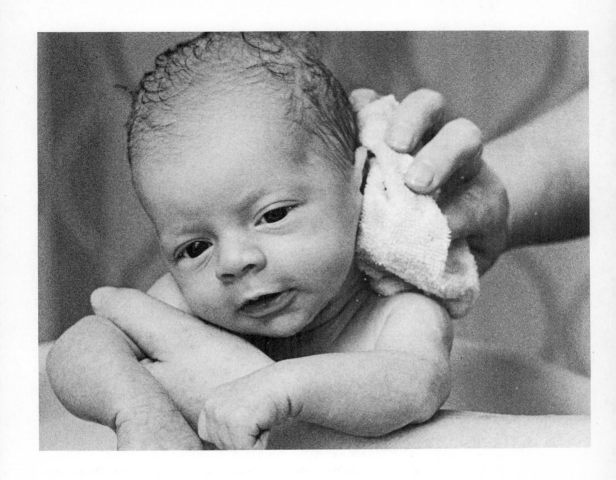

THE BABY'S NIGHTS AT THE HOSPITAL

In the past, there was no question where the baby would spend nights. Because babies were born at home, the baby spent the night at home, near the mother. Nowadays, babies are born in the hospital. Hospitals are usually divided into rooms and nurseries. For this reason, the baby spends most of the time in the nursery, and is brought to the mother when necessary. In some cases, mother and child occupy the same room.

Separation of mother and child gives the mother a chance to sleep undisturbed and to recover from the delivery of the baby. The baby is brought in at feeding time and then returned to the nursery.

This system works particularly well if more than one mother is in a room. It allows the hospital to handle the situation efficiently.

In some hospitals, the baby is permitted to spend the day and night in the same room as the mother. In order to do this successfully, the mother must be able to meet the child's needs, and there should be no more than two mothers in a room. A private room is even more preferable in this situation.

APGAR SCORING

Perhaps you have heard people discussing Apgar scores. These scores, named for the doctor who developed them, are based on a numerical assessment of five given traits of a baby. The exam is performed at 1 and 5 minutes after the child is born. A maximum of 2 points can be given for each trait. One point means that the item being tested is somewhat under normal, and a score of 0 means that the baby is seriously deficient in an area. The maximum score is 10. The lower the score, the more areas of difficulty there are.

The items that are tested are:

Skin color

Heartbeat

Respiration

Muscle tone

Reflex irritability (based on the response to a catheter in the nostril or a slap on the foot)

Two points maximum can be given to each trait, making a top score of 10 possible. On the opposite page is a chart summarizing the test.

The Apgar scores are a starting point for evaluating the condition of the child immediately after birth. They provide a basis for gauging the child's development during the next few days. Many babies have some subnormal characteristics at birth, and then come up to normal during the following days. A prognostic element exists, but it is best simply to regard the score as an assessment of the child's condition during the first few minutes of life. The information is more useful if two doctors see the child during this time. The test also provides a way to assess clearly the child's situation at birth. The most important function is to provide a basis for further observation and prognosis.

TABLE 6.1
Apgar Scoring

	0	1	2
Skin color	Paler or bluish	Body pink, extremities blue	Body and extremities pink
Heartbeat	Absent	Below 100 beats per minute	Above 100 beats per minute
Respiration	Absent	Slow and irregular	Normal, with a normal cry
Muscle tone	Completely limp	Some flexion of extremities	Well flexed
Reflex irritability	Absence of response	Grimace	Cough or sneeze or withdrawal of foot

GUTHRIE'S TEST

Before you leave the hospital a few drops of blood will be removed from your baby's heel. The blood will be dropped on special filter paper to test for phenylketonuria, which is a disease resulting from the body's inability to oxydize phenylalanine, a common compound in natural proteins. After the baby has been drinking milk for a few days, the unoxydized phenylalanine accumulates if the child has the disease. When this begins to happen, the test will show that the child is not processing phenylalanine.

If the disease is not discovered, the nervous system will be affected. It won't be noticed that the nervous system is developing incorrectly until damage has occurred. The resulting damage can cause severe mental retardation.

Fortunately, early detection will prevent this from happening. When the disease is discovered, the baby is simply put on a diet that doesn't contain natural proteins. The problem does not develop, and the child grows up normally.

Phenylketonuria is a hereditary trait that is tied to a recessive gene. Both parents must carry the gene, but neither may be affected by the disease. Families with the gene have a 1 in 4 chance of passing it on. It is distributed equally between the sexes, and occurs in 1 in 40,000 births in the United States.

7

For centuries breast feeding was the only way to feed infants. Today, however, mothers of newborns may opt to feed their children from the bottle as either a primary or supplementary feeding method. Either method, performed correctly, has its advantages and drawbacks.

BREAST FEEDING

Like so many aspects of child rearing, breast feeding is surrounded by myths. For example, family members sometimes feel that their "family" does not produce good milk, usually because the effects of one incident or another (perhaps a cold or measles) have been blown out of proportion. Do not let family rumors influence your decision. As another example, some mothers think they must "eat for two" when breast feeding. In fact, a woman may eat normally while nursing, and she does not have to put on excess weight.

In actuality, breast feeding has many practical, nutritional, and psychological advantages for both mothers and children. As a result of an increasing awareness of its benefits, more and more women today are choosing breast feeding over bottle feeding.

From the mother's point of view, it is very practical. As anyone who has had a child knows, newborns have to eat very frequently. Any measure that makes the feedings easier lightens the workload considerably. Breast milk is produced on demand at any hour and at the correct temperature. There are no problems with storage or contamination. The preparation necessary for bottle feeding is eliminated; mothers are thus relieved of the worry about the

Feeding Your Child

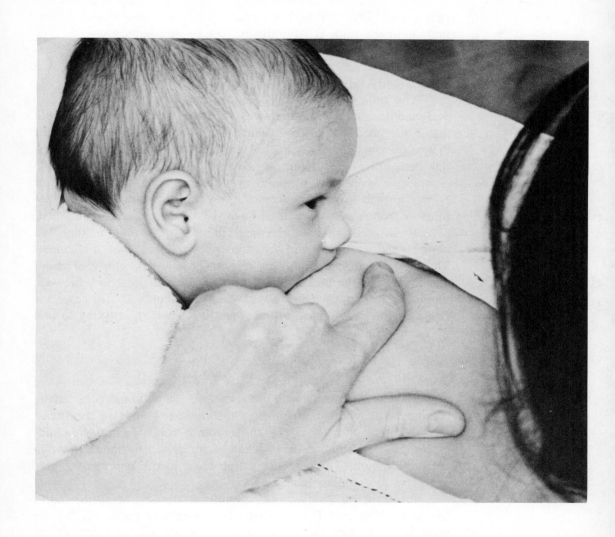

correct amount and the frustration of having to prepare formulas at irregular times of the day and night. When the baby cries for food, you simply feed him or her, and the infant quiets down and goes back to sleep.

The child also benefits. For one thing, the baby spends more time crying while the mother prepares a bottle. Perhaps more important, mother's milk is naturally perfect for the baby's system. The milk congeals into fine threads in the newborn's stomach, facilitating digestion and stimulating digestive enzymes. Thus the milk passes easily through the child's digestive tract.

The milk itself has many nutritional advantages. Specifically designed for human requirements, the food elements in the milk match the needs of the child perfectly. It contains all the nutrients that a growing infant needs. For example, iron, which is an essential element in hemoglobin, is tied to a protein that permits it to be completely assimilated by the baby's system. All the ingredients for energy growth (especially cerebral growth) are present, such as vitamins and other substances that have not yet been clearly identified.

Breast feeding also enhances the bond between mother and child. Feeding times are occasions for intimacy and tenderness. Thus feeding plays a significant role in forming ties with your child, and nursing at the breast provides a special biological link between mother and child after the baby has left the womb. It also eases the stress on the baby during a time when the newborn is trying to find its natural eating rhythm.

How Milk Is Formed in the Breast

During pregnancy, the mammary gland undergoes many changes: The volume of the breast increases, glands in the breast are activated, and the areola and nipple become darker. At childbirth, the expulsion of the placenta disrupts the hormonal flow in the bloodstream. This hormonal drop leads to the secretion of prolactin by the pituitary gland.

Prolactin ultimately causes the milk to flow by about the fourth day after childbirth. For the first day, no milk is produced. By the second, the breasts swell and begin to secrete a clear liquid called *colostrum*. This swelling continues throughout the third day, and the colostrum becomes abundant by the fourth or fifth day. By the fifth day, milk production begins, and the colostrum takes on a whiter color. The milk completely replaces the colostrum between the tenth and fifteenth days.

Why the colostrum? Its chemical composition differs from that

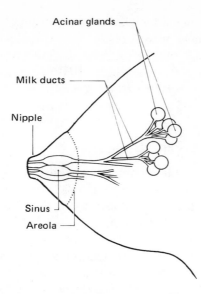

Acinar glands

Milk ducts

Nipple

Sinus

Areola

of milk. Formed in the breasts prior to childbirth, colostrum is lower in fats and sugar than milk. The gradual transition from colostrum to milk is therefore a transition from a diet that is low in fats and sugars but high in protein, to one that is high in fats and sugars but low in protein.

Once the milk starts to flow, it is kept flowing by what is called a *neurohormonal process,* that is, a process in which nerve impulses and hormones both play roles. Besides the glands, cells, and sinuses that make milk flow possible, the human breast contains many sensitive nerve endings. When a baby sucks at the breast, these nerve endings transmit a signal to the pituitary gland through the hypothalamus section of the brain. The "message" is to secrete prolactin into the bloodstream. When this hormone reaches the breast, which has been prepared to receive it, milk secretion begins.

The nerve impulses caused by the baby's sucking "tell" the pituitary gland to release another hormone, called *oxytocin*, into the bloodstream. When this hormone reaches the breasts, it contracts the acinar glands, which store and produce milk. This contraction forces milk into the milk ducts through intermediary cells, called myoepithelial cells, which surround the glands and canals. It also pushes milk forward to the nipple, where it is available to the baby. This contracting action is called the *let-down reflex.*

This reflex allows the baby to drink most of the contents of the breast. If the reflex is inhibited for any reason, the child cannot get enough milk, despite vigorous sucking. An unsatisfactory let-down reflex can also lead to engorgement, which also obstructs the flow of milk. Administering oxytocin to mothers nasally, to release the milk, is an experiment whose results vary from person to person.

Oxytocin plays another role: It causes the uterus to return to its original size. While breast feeding for the first few times, you may notice contractions similar to labor contractions. These result from the chemical action of oxytocin in the uterus.

How the Baby Extracts the Milk

Contrary to popular opinion, sucking is not the primary method that the child uses to obtain milk. Films of nursing babies show that other mechanisms are also used. First, the baby takes the nipple and areola into the mouth and compresses it with the gums to isolate it from the breast. The child's tongue presses the nipple to the roof of the mouth; successive compressions of the tongue expel milk from the sinuses into the child's mouth. After each compression the baby loosens the jaw slightly to allow the sinuses to fill up again with milk. Suction *helps* the milk to flow, but it is not of primary importance.

Nursing in the Hospital

By the second day of life, the baby is ready to eat, and you may begin nursing. Since both you and your baby are learning a new skill, remember to be patient with yourself and your infant.

Prop yourself up with pillows to a lying–sitting position. Clean the nipples of both breasts with warm, soapy water, and then rinse them with clear, warm water. Place the baby in the cradle of your arm. If you are nursing on the left side, tilt your body to the left; if nursing on the right side, tilt to the right. The baby's body will then fit comfortably against yours.

Present the breast to the baby, and place the extended nipple near the baby's mouth. Do not push the baby's head into the breast. To encourage the infant, brush the child's lips with the nipple, and place the child's tongue *above* the nipple. In response, the baby's head should turn toward you, and the mouth should open in an attempt to find the breast. To help the baby, hold the breast behind the nipple, with one finger pressing down on the upper portion. Avoid bumping the infant's nose against the breast. The child should soon seize both the nipple and a part of the areola, placing the tongue under the nipple. Light compression at the base of the breast aids the milk flow.

If during nursing the baby seems uncomfortable, stop the feed-

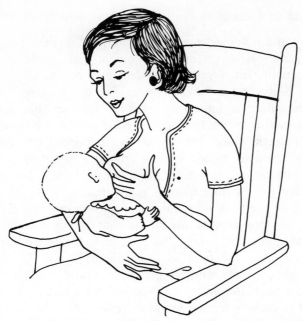

ing gently by placing your index finger between the breast and the corner of the child's mouth and gingerly nudging out the nipple. Then burp the baby. When the child has had enough, he or she will probably drink a bit more to empty the breast and then release it.

During that first week, use both breasts at each feeding, allowing the baby to nurse alternately for a few minutes at each. For one thing, even though newborns drink only small amounts, satisfying their hunger usually requires the contents of both breasts, since they contain only small quantities anyway. Through the neurohormonal process, however, each feeding encourages increased milk production. You should therefore foster equal milk flow in both breasts by offering both to the baby during this important time.

When you are using both breasts, let the baby suck from each for 5 to 10 minutes. Wait until the child has sucked most of the milk from the first breast, and then offer the second one. Leave the baby on the second breast for about 5 to 10 minutes. Do not permit nursing for more than 10 minutes on each side. When you and the child become accustomed to breast feeding and when your milk flow is well established (usually by the second week), you may want to use one breast per feeding. The reason is that with increased milk production one breast is usually sufficient to satisfy the child's hunger. If it is not, offer the other breast, but the infant will probably fall asleep before emptying it. If so, make sure to empty it yourself, using the manual method described in a later section.

Nursing at Home

Once you are home from the hospital, the feeding procedure is much the same. However, the excitement and bustle of coming home can actually interfere with the let-down reflex. Of initial concern, then, is finding a suitable place for the feedings. A quiet, relaxed atmosphere is important—despite the fact that you might have seen a mother breast feeding her child amidst a busy air terminal or other hectic place. Privacy is also important for many individuals. For example, breast feeding around a group of people can be intimidating enough to inhibit the let-down reflex. You may also feel uncomfortable about exposing your breasts to people who are not members of the immediate family, a tension that can also inhibit milk flow. A calm area of the house that is not affected by the comings and goings of family and friends is the best for nursing.

Why the need for such an atmosphere? Since the nerve impulses that stimulate the pituitary gland are routed through the hypothalamus section of the brain, this section has a direct effect on the secretion of hormones for the let-down reflex. As other stimuli—the presence of strangers, sudden loud noises, and the like—send other signals through the hypothalamus, the secretion of the necessary hormones and consequently the flow of milk can be inhibited.

Once you select an appropriate location, find a comfortable armchair or rocking chair, and leave it in the nursing area. Make sure the chair is not too low and that you can get into and out of it easily.

When you plan to feed your baby, wash your hands a little more than when you were in the hospital, and wash your breasts as before. Be gentle when you pick up the child, so as not to startle the infant. Once you are seated, place the elbow holding the baby on the chair's arm, and hold a diaper in the other hand or nearby for any burping up of milk.

Timing the Feedings

Since the baby is establishing a feeding rhythm during the first week, short and frequent feedings are desirable. Offer to feed the baby whenever he or she cries, even if you have to do so up to ten times a day. If the baby does not cry regularly, offer the child your breast every 3 hours or so. Some children adopt a schedule of being fed every 4 hours, instead of 3. If your child does so, make sure that the feedings are abundant enough to satisfy the child's nutritional needs for the longer intervals between feedings.

In most cases, the feedings level off to seven a day by the end of that first week. This schedule ordinarily entails about six feedings at 3-hour intervals during the day, around 6 A.M., 9 A.M., noon, 3 P.M., 6 P.M., and 9 or 10 P.M. The night schedule normally involves one or two feedings: the first some time between midnight and 2 A.M. and the second around 3 A.M. (You should never refuse a night feeding to a newborn who cries for it.) As far as possible, let the infant find his or her own rhythm and hours.

You do not, however, have to let the schedule control your every moment. For one thing, you do not have to stick to the hours initiated by the hospital if they do not fit into your own schedule. Those hours are instituted by the hospital to meet its organizational needs. Neither do you have to let your baby's cries completely dominate your own schedule. As you see what the baby's natural schedule is, you can adjust it to fit your own. If the baby is waking sooner than you want, give the child a few teaspoonfuls of glucose water. This technique delays the feeding for about 20 minutes. If you take this measure for the three evening feedings, you can push the whole schedule ahead by about an hour. At the end of the night feeding, give a teaspoon of sweetened condensed milk, which prolongs digestion and adds to the volume of milk to be digested. The next feeding will then come a little later than usual.

As you might expect, however, not all infants fall into a convenient pattern. Each baby has a different style of nursing. Some, for instance, wake up crying promptly on schedule and seize the breast instantly. They nurse quickly, oblivious to everything going on around them. If you interrupt their feeding, they protest violently by crying and waving their arms and legs. After taking as much milk as they want, they burp contentedly and fall back to sleep.

Other children are so interested in the world around them that they consider nursing only a secondary activity. They may wake up crying for food, or they may wake up quietly and look around the room for a half-hour or so. When you present the breast to them, they may not take it immediately. When they finally do, they slowly take a few mouthfuls, stop to savor the flavor, and then take the breast again. As the feeding progresses, they may stop from time to time to examine the world. They stop nursing at the least sound and turn their heads to see what is happening. Such babies require a lot of patience from their mothers. The feedings are such leisurely affairs that you should find a calm area that won't interrupt the feeding too often. Speak softly to the child while nursing to preserve the quiet atmosphere, which this sort of child needs. In spite of the relaxed pace of the feeding, these children take as much milk as those who nurse more quickly.

Some babies are not interested in anything except sleeping. They rarely wake up crying. When offered the breast, they take a few swallows and then stop, as if they are discouraged by the effort required. They often fall asleep during feedings, and their mothers tend to think that they are not getting anything to eat. These babies might be easier to bottle feed than to breast feed. Your doctor can help you decide which type of formula and schedule best suits your baby. When it is impossible to stimulate a baby's appetite, a fixed amount at a particular hour may solve the problem.

When any baby sleeps beyond the scheduled feeding time, your breasts may become tender because they need to be emptied. If you think a feeding is in order, do not pick up the baby suddenly; you will only startle the child and possibly start him or her crying. Instead, pick up the infant slowly, speaking gently and brushing the lips with the nipple. The infant will probably take the nipple but continue to doze—and likely sleep to the next feeding. If your breasts are still tender, you must empty them, using the technique described later in this chapter.

Some babies are not satisfied with even your best efforts. Everything annoys them. These babies often perplex and frustrate most parents. They always wake up crying and act as if they are forever starving. They continue to cry even after being offered milk, probably because they can not find the breast quickly enough. If the milk flows too slowly or too quickly, they cry again. Some mothers are tempted to give up breast feeding such children, because they tend to think that they are at fault for the child's behavior or because, at other times, their milk production diminishes. Calm and patience are required with these babies. You must remain in control and try to make them nurse properly. Experimentation will show you a system that makes feedings bearable. (Interestingly, parents of these children are often a little "nervous" themselves, and, as infants, they often posed the same problems for their own parents.)

Other babies are so good that they amaze their parents. They wake up content, and they play with their hands or stare at the ceiling until you are ready for them. They take the bottle or breast calmly and drink happily. At the end of the feeding, they give you a gentle smile, burp, and go back to sleep.

As you can see, feeding routines vary from child to child. You have to get to know your own child before working out a routine of your own. Your baby might fall into one of the type-categories described, or the child might demonstrate characteristics of several types. Do not be discouraged if a routine does not readily materialize. Some are just a little harder to establish than others.

The Amount of the Feeding

Since all children are so different, the volume of milk they "should" take at each feeding is difficult to set into rules. However, one rule of thumb is that an average feeding should take about ten minutes. The baby takes most of the milk during the first five minutes and the rest in another three. Naturally, infants who drink more slowly may take up to fifteen or twenty minutes. If the quantities taken over a 24-hour period are normal, you should not be concerned about how long the feedings take or about how much is taken at each feeding. Your chief concern in this area is that evening and morning feedings are ample, since these are more important than the others.

How much is enough in the course of a day? If your milk production is normal and if the newborn is a vigorous feeder, then the following quantities are considered normal:

Day 1	Day 2	Day 3	Day 4	Day 5	Day 6	Day 7
A few grams of water or colostrum	60–90	120–150	180–250	240–300	300–400	360–500
			(Grams)			

These amounts might not be enough, however, if the nutrient content of the milk is low. If, for instance, you do not empty your breasts after each feeding, the leftover milk loses some of its nutritional content.

In general you should try to feed these amounts over a 24-hour period. How you do so, again, depends very much on the baby. Those who take more at their daytime feedings might not need both or any night feedings. Others who take less during the day might need the seventh or eighth feeding at night. Still others drink a lot of milk during the day and *still* require night feedings. Also, babies that weigh less than average at birth (below 5½ pounds) usually need the eighth feeding to compensate for the small amounts they usually take during the day; this feeding also increases the child's weight more rapidly. If your baby is within the average weight range (5½ to 8 pounds), then fewer feedings might be enough.

Conditions for Breast Feeding

To make breast feeding a healthful and satisfying choice for you and for your newborn, you must *want* to feed your baby this way. If you do not, your attitude can affect the let-down reflex and consequently the flow of milk to the baby. Some mothers resent how their clothing must be specially tailored to accommodate the feedings. Some do not want the feedings to interfere with their social or professional lives. Some find breast feeding disagreeable— or they just do not want to do it. Whatever their reasons, mothers should not undertake breast feeding if they do not want to do so. If they have to force themselves, they might be "cheating" their infants out of proper nourishment and letting themselves in for an unhappy relationship with their children.

Assuming a mother wants to breast feed her newborn, the next principal requirement is that she must be in generally good health. Any of the following medical conditions would probably rule her out as a candidate for breast feeding, although each case should be evaluated by a doctor as research continues to indicate that there are fewer and fewer absolute restrictions:

The ingestion of certain medications
Any contagious disease, such as tuberculosis
Certain endocrine disorders
Kidney infections
Nervous disorders
Blood incompatibilities with the child

Other physical conditions might not rule out breast feeding, but they can make it difficult. A common problem is an abnormality of the nipples. If the baby is sucking normally but waking up hungry before the typical three hours are up, the child is probably not getting enough to eat at the feedings. In such cases, one of two types of abnormalities might be the cause: either the nipple does not extend at all, or it does not extend when the baby is sucking. In each case, the baby cannot nurse properly. Although you might consider the use of a pump to extract the milk for the baby, which will help milk production, you just might have to bottle feed the child.

Another difficulty presents itself when nipples become cracked and sore, perhaps because the baby is taking the nipple and not the areola. This condition may also result when the baby continues to suck even after the breast is emptied. As feedings become more and more painful, milk production is often reduced. Treat this problem as soon as it develops. Your doctor will probably prescribe the application of an ointment three or four times a day.

Some women have problems with the let-down reflex or milk flow, perhaps from a lack of demand. If the milk does not flow immediately, the baby swallows excess air. The infant then stops, burps, and tries again. If the milk still does not flow, feedings turn into noisy, frustrating affairs, with gas, vomiting, and colic. The mother is often tempted to abandon breast feeding before giving it a good chance. Actually, the let-down reflex is reacting too slowly to meet the baby's needs. By the time milk flow starts, the baby is tired. The child takes a small amount and falls asleep, only to awaken a half-hour later.

The solution to this problem is easy to recommend and difficult to follow. The mother must be calm prior to and during nursing, and she must not regard success or failure at nursing as vital to her personal identity. If you remain calm, the let-down reflex has a greater chance of functioning normally. Before each feeding, massaging the breast for 5 minutes or so may help; softly rub around the areola to stimulate the reflex. If your attempts do not bring good results, bottle feeding may be the best answer for you and your baby.

When the passage of milk from the acinar glands (where it is produced) to the sinuses (where it is collected for nursing) is blocked, engorgement results. This problem may affect only one part or all of the gland. In its simplest form, engorgement causes the section around the areola to become painful and tender. Nursing, of course, becomes difficult. Emptying your breasts manually alleviates this tenderness.

If the entire gland is affected, however, the problem is more serious. The breasts are hot, red, and tender to the lightest touch. Stop nursing at least on the side that is affected, put ice packs on the breast, and contact your doctor. If engorgement is not treated, it can lead to lymphangitis. Fever develops, the breasts become more and more tender, the pain progresses to the underarm, and the veins become blue. Eventually an abscess may develop. This problem must be treated immediately.

How to Empty the Breasts Manually

As noted, the removal of excess milk from the breasts is essential for two reasons:

1. When milk stays in the breasts for a certain period, some of its nutrients are reabsorbed by the body. The next time your baby nurses, the milk contains less nutrition. The milk becomes more transparent, resembling colostrum in some ways.

2. If the breasts are not emptied, milk production decreases, because the body adjusts supply to demand.

Emptying your breasts is easy, but it takes a few attempts to develop the knack. Basically, you must move the milk from the acinar glands, at the base of the breasts where the milk is produced, through the milk ducts to the sinuses in the areola, where it can then be manually pressed out of the breast.

To prepare, you must wash your hands thoroughly and have in front of you a sterile jar or other kind of suitable receptacle.

The first step is to move the milk up to the sinuses. To do so, place your palms flat on your chest with your fingers resting downward on your breast. Press the back portion of the breast a few times, to move the milk from the acinar glands to the sinuses.

The next step is to empty the milk into the jar or receptacle. Place your hands again on your chest, but position your fingers at the base of the breasts. Press inward toward the interior of the breasts about ten times. After doing so, you will notice that the sinuses of the nipple are distended with milk.

Finally, take the sterile receptacle in one hand, and place the

thumb and index finger of the other hand just behind the brown section of the breast. Press from the interior of the breast to the nipple. After a few compressions, the milk will squirt from the breast. Do the same with the other breast. (The milk may be stored in the refrigerator, but cover the jar tightly.)

This technique may be used the first few weeks to stimulate milk production, but you should need it less and less as time goes on. If, after 10 or 15 days, your milk flow is not well established, give the child both breasts as often as possible. If the infant is not taking all the milk, drain your breasts after feedings. You can also use this technique to relieve the pressure if your breasts become too full.

As an alternative procedure, manual and electric pumps are available. They are used for inverted nipples and for extracting milk for babies who do not drink enough milk otherwise.

Breast Feeding and Medication

Many women wonder whether it is safe to take any medication while breast feeding their children. In some cases it is; in some it is not. Most antibiotics are passed into the milk. If, however, the duration and dosages are not excessive, you may, quite likely, be able to continue nursing. Sometimes the antibiotic gives the milk a sour taste, and the baby may refuse it; others may take it but have digestive problems. If your illness requires long-term treatment, you might have to discontinue nursing. You and your doctor should consider each situation individually.

BOTTLE FEEDING

Sometimes bottle feeding is preferable to nursing. Perhaps the mother is too sick to breast feed her baby, or perhaps she has a problem with the let-down reflex, or perhaps her nipples are too sensitive to permit nursing. Also, as noted, if the mother does not want to nurse the child for any reason, she should consider bottle feeding. A smooth bottle-feeding system is by far preferable to a badly managed, annoying nursing routine.

Certainly no mother should feel that she is shortchanging her newborn by choosing the bottle-feeding method. Formulas for bottle feeding so closely approximate the composition of breast milk that babies fed on those formulas grow just as fast as those who are fed

breast milk. Bottle feeding also meets the child's need for intimacy, as long as the mother feeds the baby with calmness and joy.

Formulas

Which formula is best for your child? Your doctor can help you select a suitable one, since many factors influence your decision. Your child's weight, appetite, and digestive system must all be considered. For example, babies who are colicky require formulas that are different from those for babies who digest their food rapidly. The frequency of bowel movements is also a factor. Furthermore, as your baby grows, his or her needs change, and you must periodically reevaluate the formula to determine whether it is the right kind and whether the quantity is sufficient.

Many commercial formulas are available, but they can be divided into three general categories, depending on how the basic cow's milk is modified for feeding to infants. (Cow's milk alone does not contain the same proportions of nutrients as mother's milk.)

1. *Basic milk* is cow's milk with a lot of the fat removed. Usually in powdered form, it has sugar added.
2. *Basic milks with additional nutrients* resemble mother's milk more closely than basic milk. For example, some have a simplified form of sugar that is more digestible for the baby than regular sugar and that is chemically similar to the sugars found in breast milk. Fats from vegetable sources may also be added since cow's milk is low in nonsaturated acid fats, which are essential to the baby's growth. Finally, because the proteins found in cow's milk (casein) are not as digestible as those found in mother's milk, acid is sometimes added to break those proteins down into simpler, more digestible forms.
3. *Modified and enriched formulas* contain sugars, fats, modified proteins, and salts, but they also contain vitamins and iron to make them resemble human milk more closely.

Formulas come in a variety of forms:

1. *Powdered:* Most often used, some are "acidified" to dissolve in cold or lukewarm water. Nonacidified powders must be reconstituted in hot water.
2. *Liquid concentrate:* These are sometimes sweetened and homogenized.
3. *Liquid (ready-to-use):* These formulas are not widely used except in hospitals.

Bottles and Nipples

Several problems can develop with the mechanics of bottle feeding, most of which are not serious and are easily solved with a little experimentation.

Types of Bottles Of the many different materials and types of bottles on the market, most are well tested, but their characteristics vary greatly. Consequently, you should consider which best meets your needs before settling on a choice.

In the past, a glass bottle with a stretch nipple was popular. This type is not often used today because it is more difficult to sterilize than modern bottles, and because it permits the baby to swallow a lot of air.

Another type, currently very popular, is the glass or plastic bottle with a nipple that snaps into a ring-style cap. While caps and bottles can be sterilized together, glass bottles are sterilized more quickly, but plastic is lighter. Small and large sizes are available. The small size is convenient for the first week, after which the large size is necessary.

The caps can also be used to adjust the flow of milk by tightening or loosening the cap. The cap must not be too tight or too loose. If too tight, the cap causes a difference in air pressures between inside and outside the bottle, which impedes milk flow. Consequently, the infant tires quickly, due to the extra effort needed to get the milk. If the cap is too loose, milk flow increases, sometimes to the point where the baby cannot swallow it all. Choking and coughing are signs of this problem. Experimentation will show you how tight you should make the bottle cap. If your baby is a vigorous eater, tighten the ring a bit more than you might normally. If your baby is a relaxed eater, loosen the cap slightly.

Disposable bottles are undergoing experimentation in some countries. They contain a ready-to-use, sterilized formula. The mother has only to put on the nipple and heat the bottle. They are very practical, especially for babies of low birth weight who require germ-free milk.

Some bottles have been designed to make sterilization easier and to decrease air swallowing. The bottle consists of a plastic shell, disposable plastic bags to hold the milk, and a nipple that is specially designed for the shell. The plastic bag is thrown out after each use, and the shells and nipples can be sterilized together. Measuring the milk is less precise than with conventional bottles, but it is exact enough to suit the purpose.

Types of Nipples   Although bottles may be comparable in quality, nipples have different characteristics that may make one brand preferable to another. The hole in the nipple must be the right size to permit a smooth flow of milk. If the hole is too small, the baby has to work hard to get the milk. If the hole is too big, the milk flows into the baby's mouth too quickly, and the child must turn away to cough out the excess.

Nipples may be bought either pierced or unpierced. The unpierced types may seem to have an advantage because presumably you can make the holes exactly as big or as small as you want. However, making the holes exactly right can be difficult for some people, so they might prefer the prepierced types. On the other hand, the prepierced holes might be too large for some babies and too small for others. To find out if they are an acceptable size, turn the bottle upside down: A short jet of milk should come out, followed by only a few drops of milk.

Some companies offer a nipple whose hole size adjusts according to position. These nipples are less easily stopped up by lumps than conventional nipples, but even these are sometimes not large enough for a healthy eater.

Probably the best thing for you to do is to experiment with several different styles to see which suits your needs best. If your child is a vigorous eater, select nipples that are firm and that have small holes. If your baby's appetite varies from feeding to feeding, the style with the adjustable hole may be best. A razor cut may be necessary to open the prefabricated hole slightly.

Sterilization Procedures

Generally, you should have enough sterile bottles on hand for one day, and you might want to have an extra one around for fruit juices. Since most sterilizers have spaces for only seven bottles, you might have to take steps to provide that extra bottle or two.

Terminal Sterilization   With this method, you prepare an entire day's supply of bottles at one time. The procedure consists of two phases: (1) preparing the formula and (2) preparing the sterilized bottles.

To prepare the formula, the following measures are necessary:

1. Line up the washed and dried bottles on a clean surface.
2. Put the necessary amount of water in each bottle (according to the manufacturer's instructions).
3. Measure out the correct amount of powdered or concentrated formula into each bottle.
4. Close the bottles.
5. Shake the bottles to dissolve and mix the formula. You may also mix the entire batch in a clean bowl, and pour it into each bottle.

The next phase is to sterilize the bottles:

1. If you have mixed the formula in a bowl, wash and dry the bottles before filling them. Turn the nipples upside down into the neck of the bottle. Place the plastic cap into the ring, and screw it about halfway onto the bottle. This looseness permits vapor to escape while the bottles are being sterilized.

2. Place the bottles in a sterilization pan with about 2½ to 3 inches of water in it.
3. Put the cover on, and boil for about 20 minutes.
4. Let the bottles cool in the sterilizer. Leave the cover on during cooling.
5. Open the sterilizer, and tighten the rings to obtain a sterile closing of the bottle.
6. Put the bottles in the refrigerator.
7. Reheat the bottle in a pan of hot water when you are going to use it.

Aseptic Method   In this second method, the empty bottles are first sterilized and then filled with formula as needed. First the bottles must be sterilized:

1. Wash and dry the bottles, and place them in the sterilizer.
2. Fill the sterilizer according to the manufacturer's instructions, and boil for 10 minutes.
3. Let the bottles cool, and then take the cover off the sterilizer.

When you are ready to use a bottle, follow these steps:

1. Wash your hands.
2. Open the sterile bottle, trying not to touch the inside of the bottle with your fingers.
3. Put the nipple into the cap, and rest both on a clean surface.
4. Fill the bottle with the necessary amounts of water and formula (according to the manufacturer's instructions).
5. Place the bottle in the warmer. If you are using acidified milk, warm it more thoroughly.

Advantages and Disadvantages   Naturally, each method has its pros and cons. Terminal sterilization is the more sterile, and it does not leave the preparation of bottles up to inexperienced persons such as babysitters. Also, the formula need be prepared only once a day. (In the past, preparing the milk was a bigger task than it is today. You had to boil and dilute the cow's milk, add sugar and flour to it, and then strain it to remove lumps.) The terminal method also allows you to use tap water, because the formula is sterilized.

This method also has some disadvantages. For one thing, the shock of heat to the milk alters the structures of the proteins. (Most formulas have already had their proteins altered by one or two prior sterilizations.) Also, when the milk boils in the bottles, a residue collects in the neck of the bottles, which may plug up the holes of the nipples, since they are turned into the bottlenecks.

The aseptic method is more widely used today. Instant formulas dissolve quickly, and bottles do not become clogged. The protein structures are not changed, because the formula is not boiled. (You may want to boil the water also for the first few months, to make sure that it is germ free.)

Other Sterilization Requirements After using a bottle, you must take precautions, or nothing will be sterilized. Wash the bottles and nipples with soapy water and with bottle and nipple brushes— immediately after use. Do not wait to do all of them at the end of the day. After the bottles and nipples are washed, place them under a cloth to protect them from dust and insects. Keep everything in a clean area of your kitchen.

You need several utensils for washing and sterilizing:

1. A bottle brush that is the diameter of your bottles,
2. A nipple brush,
3. Tongs to manipulate the bottles, and
4. A pot in which to keep the used bottles.

Of course, you need a sterilizer as well. Of the many boil-type models on the market, most are equivalent in quality. Less widely used is the chemical sterilizer, which uses chlorine. With a chemical sterilizer, wash the bottles and nipples thoroughly with soap and brushes. Separate the bottles, nipples, and rings. Immerse all of them into the solution, making sure that no air bubbles are in the nipples or bottles. Put the lid on the sterilizer, and make certain that everything is submerged in the solution. When you are ready to use a bottle, put the nipple into the ring, after washing everything carefully with boiled or mineral water. Let the bottles dry for a few minutes before putting everything together. Then add your formula.

You need not, however, go out and buy a sterilizer. You may also use a pressure cooker. Simply put the empty, closed, and clean bottles in with the nipples reversed into the necks of the bottles. Pour in 2½ to 3 inches of water, put on the valve, and boil for 7 to 10 minutes. (Make sure the valve is positioned to release steam.)

An electric oven also serves as an acceptable sterilizer for at least the bottles. Place the open and empty bottles on the oven rack. Turn the oven up to 212°–248° F (100°–120° C), and keep it there for 6 to 8 minutes. After turning the oven off, let the bottles cool in it. As you do the bottles in the oven, boil the nipples and rings on the range for no more than 3 minutes (more boiling can damage the rubber). An oven cannot be used for plastic bottles.

Timing of Bottle Feedings

Many of the rules and cautions that apply to nursing pertain also to bottle feeding. Newborns generally need to be fed every 3 hours and once at night. While the six day feedings are normally conducted on a predetermined schedule, the baby usually lets you know by crying when the night feeding should take place. Try to get these feedings on a regular schedule, especially the night feeding, to make your life easier. By the same token, do not become obsessed with a rigid schedule. Your baby may not have to eat exactly every 180 minutes; variations of a quarter-hour or so are perfectly normal.

You might want to adjust your baby's schedule slightly. For example, if the feeding times established by the hospital do not suit your schedule, you can modify them according to your needs. To make the next feeding a little earlier, dilute the formula in the current feeding; that is, mix a little less than the usual amount of formula with the normal amount of water. If you want to move the night feeding forward an hour, give a few teaspoonfuls of glucose water when the baby wakes up for food. This technique delays the present feeding for about 20 minutes. If you do this for the three feedings preceding the night feeding, the night feeding will be delayed by about one hour.

If the baby is regularly waking up about a half-hour before the scheduled feedings, the child is not getting enough nourishment. Increase the amount of formula at each feeding. If the baby does not wake up at the scheduled feeding time, wait for about a half-hour before waking the infant.

Consult your doctor before making any changes in the schedule.

Demand or Directed Feeding?

Should babies be fed according to schedule or as they cry for food? This question highlights the difference between demand or directed (scheduled) feeding. Demand feeding advocates state that the baby should be fed every time he or she cries because any other way is unnatural and unnecessarily frustrating to the child. Supporters of directed feeding maintain that a scheduled approach encourages optimum growth and avoids stomach problems.

The background of these two schools of thought might help you to evaluate them. In days gone by, such controversies did not exist. Breast-fed babies sucked whenever they wanted, and they sucked as much as they wanted. During those times, intestinal problems played a major role in infant mortality rates. Attempts to adapt cow's milk to infant needs by adding water and sugar often led to fatal bouts of diarrhea.

Formula milks gradually were developed in an attempt to eliminate this problem. Cow's milk and the water added to it were sterilized, and the resultant formula was placed in sterile bottles. Combinations of water and milk were calculated very carefully to avoid digestive problems. In the beginning, however, the results were not very satisfactory. The occurrence of digestive problems among babies who were on formula was much higher than among those who were on breast milk, because the quality of the cow's milk varied considerably.

The success of formula feeding depended greatly on sticking to a strict schedule. In time, the idea of feeding children on a schedule was applied also to breast feeding. A schedule, it was thought, would help avoid digestion disorders in nursing babies as well. As the years went by, schedules became a part of unquestioned dogma.

During the last twenty years or so, the field of pediatrics and the formula industry have simultaneously made great advances. Fatal intestinal problems have become almost nonexistent. Major digestive disorders have come to be handled fairly routinely. The problems of breast and bottle feeding have been worked out.

Consequently, theorists have come around full circle. The most recent theory, developed by a psychologist and pediatrician, states that babies should be fed whenever they cry for food. During the first few weeks, the baby calls for milk many times and at irregular intervals. Then during the third week, the baby levels out to about six feedings roughly 3 to 4 hours apart. This method is called demand feeding.

Although applicable to either nursed or bottle-fed babies, demand feeding is not practical for all babies, mothers, and circumstances. It absolutely cannot be used with premature and low-birth-weight children. Nor can it be used with infants who do not cry for their feedings or with those who wake up at every sound and who have short sleeping periods. The mother must also be able to differentiate between cries that occur because of hunger and those that result from other needs—relief from boredom, a change of diapers, a little affection. Obviously, a baby who is fed everytime he or she cries for any reason is quickly going to be overfed.

Finally, although the child might be a good candidate for

demand feeding, the mother might not. If the baby's schedule does not fit well with that of the parents, demand feeding can create anarchy in the home. For example, the mother might have to resume a career. Some mothers simply do not choose to assume responsibility for this sort of program.

So if you are considering this type of feeding, consult your doctor. You and your doctor must take several factors into account: your baby's personality, health, birth weight, and sleeping schedule, as well as your lifestyle, personality, and available time. The baby must have a normal appetite and sleep patterns, and you must be willing and able to handle this type of schedule. During the first week, feeding is quite irregular. By the second week, the baby should be encouraged to eat roughly every 3 hours. Try to guide the child toward a schedule that best suits your routine, in consultation with your physician. You will probably arrive at a schedule that fits your daily life and that is still not too rigid.

Whichever method you choose, avoid extremes. A directed method does not mean that the baby has to be fed at the exact minute prescribed by the schedule. Your child might wake up a little early or late. Also, use the prescribed amounts as guidelines, not as inflexible rules.

The Correct Amount of Formula

Your doctor will advise you on the correct amount of formula and on suitable increases as the baby grows. For instance, some doctors dilute the formula more during the first month than in following months. Others prefer to give the formula full strength during this period; they think that the energy needs of the newborn warrant full strength.

For your general information, however, here are a few general rules of thumb. When you leave the hospital, the baby needs at least seven bottles, each containing about 2 to 3 ounces, every day. By fifteen days, increase the amount given to 3 to 3½ ounces. By the third week, 3½ to 4 ounces are required. Another helpful guideline is to calculate the number of ounces by adding 2 or 3 to the baby's age in months. For example, if the infant is under one month old, 2 or 3 ounces are needed at each feeding. If the infant is two months old, 4 or 5 ounces are need.

Bear in mind, however, that appetites vary in children as they do in adults, and you must adjust these "rules" to suit your child's appetite. Your personal experience and your doctor's advice will help you along the way.

Besides varying from child to child, a baby's appetite might also change from day to day and from morning to night. For instance, infants normally take more formula at their morning and night feedings than they do in their afternoon sessions. Also, if after the bottle is empty, the baby cries, sucks the fingers, or wakes up early for the next feeding, then the child is probably not getting enough nourishment. If in such a case you feel you should increase the amount of the feeding, you may safely add a half-ounce while waiting for the recommendation of the doctor. You must take care, however, since overfeeding can make sleep more difficult and create digestive problems.

Temperature of the Bottle

Bottle temperature is a debated question in the pediatric field. Heating the bottle to around 98° F seems logical, because this is the temperature of mother's milk. Yet experience has shown that a majority of infants prefer a warmer temperature. Experience has also compelled some doctors to recommend giving bottles at room temperature or lower; some babies do not seem to mind their bottles at this temperature.

You have to experiment to find out which temperature best suits your infant. You can check the temperature by dropping a bit of milk on your wrist. If it feels comfortable, the bottle is probably warm enough. You should always check the temperature before giving the bottle to the baby.

Bottle Feeding Procedure

As with breast feeding, find a calm place in the house to feed the baby. Make sure that the chair is comfortable, and have a clean diaper or towel ready in case you need it. Wash your hands thoroughly before starting.

Hold the baby, as if you were breast feeding, in the crook of your arm and close to your body. The baby's head should be resting inside your elbow. Brush the baby's lips open with the nipple. When the baby opens his or her mouth, put the nipple in. Don't force the baby's mouth open by putting your fingers between the gums or by pinching the jaws. Make sure that the bottle is at the right temperature and that the flow is correct. Tilt the bottle slightly to avoid letting air enter the nipple.

Babies take their bottles in different ways. Some start by taking half the bottle, sleep a few minutes, burp, and then cry for

the remainder; they then finish the bottle less urgently than at the start of the feeding. If your child follows this pattern, keep the bottle warm in a pan of hot water while the baby dozes. Other children may take the feeding all at once, and still others have a more leisurely approach.

Keep an eye on the bottle as the feeding progresses. Do not let the nipple collapse while the baby is sucking. If it does, the cap is probably on too tight. The baby cannot suck the milk out because a vacuum has formed in the bottle. The milk that is sucked out is replaced by air, and the nipple caves in because of the outside pressure.

Even if the nipple does not collapse, tiny air bubbles must flow into the bottle as milk leaves it. If the baby is sucking and you cannot see these bubbles, then the hole is blocked. The baby is swallowing only air. Some babies cry when they do not get the milk, but the majority do not. Dislodge the obstruction by pressing hard on the tip of the nipple. However, do not interrupt feedings frequently to check the nipple hole.

If the baby falls back into a deep sleep after finishing only half the bottle, the hole of the nipple may be too small or the cap too tight. In either case, the work of obtaining the milk is too much for the baby, who tires of the effort. If you adjust the hole and the cap and if your baby still does not drink a typical amount, call your doctor. This situation is not normal.

If the baby is having difficulty swallowing the milk, too much is flowing into the child's mouth. The bubbles in the bottle are larger than normal, and either the cap is too loose or the nipple hole is too big.

There are a few practices that you should avoid. Do not lay the bottle horizontally on the baby while he or she is lying in the crib. This angle directs the flow of milk toward the upper portion of the nasal cavities. If the milk flows into the nasal cavities and particularly into the eustachian tube, an inflammation of the ear can easily develop. Also, do not prop up the bottle in the crib so that the baby can take the bottle alone. This position is dangerous to a small baby.

SUPPLEMENTING BREAST FEEDING WITH BOTTLE FEEDING

If the newborn is not getting enough nourishment, you might have to either stimulate milk production or complete the feeding from the bottle. Give the baby the breast (5 minutes on each side), and then follow with as much formula as the baby wants. You might have to increase the amount of formula until your milk production catches up to the baby's needs. If for some reason the baby falls asleep at the breast after only a few sucks, you might give the child a bottle of breast milk that has been extracted manually. If your flow is not enough to fill a bottle, feed the baby for 5 minutes on each side, and supplement the feeding with formula until the third or fourth day. In the meantime, use a breast pump to stimulate production.

BURPING THE BABY

After drinking for 5 or 10 minutes, the baby sucks less vigorously and may soon need to burp up the air taken in while feeding. The amount of swallowed air varies from baby to baby: Some swallow very little air, while others do not have to burp because the shapes of their stomachs accommodate the swallowed air. Burping usually occurs spontaneously a few minutes—sometimes a little longer— after feeding. To help the baby bring up the air, use one of the following techniques:

1. Hold the baby vertically on your shoulder, and pat the child's back rhythmically.

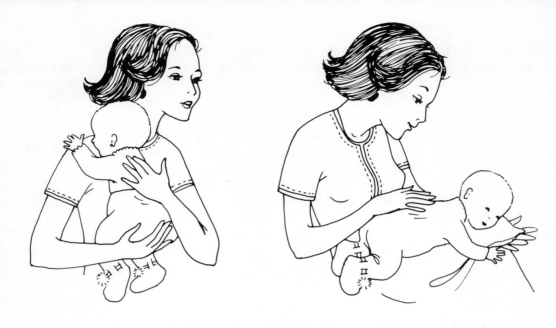

2. Sit the infant on your knees, with your hand supporting the head. Pat the baby's back gently with the other hand.
3. Lay the baby flat on your knees, with your hand supporting the head. The baby should lie on his or her stomach, with the head turned to one side. Pat gently and rhythmically on the back.

Any one of these techniques usually yields a burp. Have a diaper or washcloth under the baby's chin, because a small quantity of milk often comes up with the burp. If the baby does not seem to need to burp or does not burp after being held for a while, let the child sleep, lying on one side.

Sometimes the baby swallows so much air that you must interrupt the feeding for a burp. If so, wait until the infant shows signs of discomfort, and do not interrupt the feeding until the baby has had a substantial amount of milk. (Some babies also hiccup after feeding—a normal occurrence.)

REGURGITATION

Regurgitation of milk at the end of a feeding is also normal. It is not traumatic for the child, and it is not to be confused with vomiting. Some of the regurgitation is only milk that has accumulated around the mouth during the feeding, and some is milk that was just swallowed.

Regurgitation is often considered a "sending back" of excess milk. You should not discourage or try to "make up" for the "lost" milk by feeding the child more. Simply prepare for it by having a towel or diaper ready. Place the cloth under the child's chin to avoid soiling your clothes or those of the baby.

During the first few days of life, the baby burps up mucus that was in the stomach during the fetal stage. The mucus is fluid and adheres to the side of the mouth. Gently clean out the mouth with a clean cloth so that the child does not swallow it again.

AFTER THE FEEDING

The baby who finishes eating usually burps and is happy. If the infant does not fall right back to sleep, use that time for a few words of "conversation." You should not let these moments pass without a warm and affectionate exchange.

Some mothers feel embarrassed and think that they have nothing to say. The words are not important. Mothers and babies have their own special type of communication in tones and words. If you cannot think of a way to get these conversations going, try to recall how you talked to your dolls when you were younger. If you did not play with dolls or if you do not remember what you said, just say what you feel to your baby: Simply say that you feel silly, that you really cannot think of a thing to say, and that the baby must have patience until you learn how to say all the things that you want to say. After a few times, the words will flow very naturally. As the days go by, you will no longer feel apprehension when the baby cries. Instead, you will look forward to the calming effect that you provide. You will enjoy the pleasant times with your new infant.

During these times, the child learns to recognize your features, and you learn the intricacies of your child's expressions. Babies' faces are very mobile. As you speak to them softly, smiles and bright expressions reward your efforts. Yet, just when you think you are really communicating, the smile turns to a frown, and the baby starts to cry. You should not feel rejected or defeated. Probably all that has happened is that the baby's diapers need a change. Your natural reaction may be that an unpleasant moment has intruded on a pleasant one. Yet what you see as an unhappy turn of events for the child is not at all what you think it is.

BOWEL MOVEMENTS

Children take pleasure in bodily functions; the infant is actually happy with what he or she produces. Consequently, you should avoid a tone of recrimination when you discover a dirty diaper, because this function is very important to the child. Since the child feels, quite normally, a pleasant satisfaction when excreting waste products, you should not make the child feel about the less pleasant aspects of this act.

The consistency of the baby's stools depends a great deal on the method of feeding. If breast fed, the baby produces stools that are clotted, soft, greenish, and sour-smelling (although not particularly offensive). If you are bottle feeding, the child's stools are compact, less clotted, less frequent, and yellowish (the color of egg yolks). Bottle-fed children produce waste products that are more easily detachable from the diaper.

Be careful not to confuse loose stools with diarrhea. Only if the child's movements are more fluid than what you consider normal for your baby should you suspect diarrhea. In the newborn, loose stools are not uncommon, particularly in the first week, when digestive habits are not altogether established. At this stage, you need not worry because pediatric nurses are trained to spot any abnormalities. These nurses also take into account the nature of the formula that the baby is ingesting.

You must monitor the number of movements in a day, which also depends, among other things, on the method of feeding and the type of formula. Bottle-fed children tend to have fewer movements than breast-fed babies; although a child on the bottle may "go" after each feeding, he or she is more likely to have a movement only three or four times a day. Milks that are high in complex sugars (such as common table sugar) are passed more slowly than those with simple sugars, such as lactose or multidextrose. If movements are too frequent, too soft, or yellow or green in color, your doctor may recommend a formula with less lactose in it. If movements are hard and small, a fast-transit milk may be substituted.

The child's temperament and hereditary features also affect the number of movements. If the parents have a problem with constipation, for instance, the child may well inherit this trait.

Green bowel movements, often a cause for alarm to the new mother, result from an oxidation of bile pigments, which turn green when exposed to air. Movements are generally yellow when first passed, but they turn green when allowed to stay in the diaper for a while. If the movement is excreted a little more rapidly than usual, the acids that remain in the stool favor oxidation. This condition is not a sign of an ailment.

Sometimes a breast-fed baby has hard and less frequent movements, often from not getting enough nourishment. Weight gain is usually below normal in such cases. Your doctor will probably suggest that you empty your breasts after each feeding to encourage milk production. Drinking more fluids and resting more often than you usually do will also help milk production.

Some babies use all the milk in digestion and do not pass any waste products; in such cases, weight gain usually remains normal. Your doctor might advise an extra bottle to aid bowel movement.

8

THE POSTPARTUM PHASE

During the postpartum phase your body will return to the state it was in before you became pregnant. This phase usually lasts about six weeks.

The uterus shrinks to a more normal size soon after childbirth. Eight days after delivery it measures about 4 inches below the navel. By the fifteenth day it has returned to the true pelvis. The uterine lining rebuilds itself between the twentieth and the forty-fifth day. The cervix closes by the tenth day. The vulva and the vagina regain their elasticity after a few days. Ovulation usually does not take place before the return of the menstrual period if the mother is not nursing. The date of the return of the menstrual cycle is more variable if the mother is nursing. Contrary to what is often believed, it is possible to ovulate and to become pregnant again while nursing. If you are not nursing, your period will probably return about 45 days after childbirth.

The mother loses the excess weight resulting from the pregnancy. The weight of the child, fluid, and the placenta have already been lost. Weight resulting from water retention will take longer to lose. After your body settles down to not being pregnant, you will know if you have gained or lost weight as a result of the pregnancy.

It is a good idea to try to be up and out of bed within 24 hours after a normal vaginal delivery. Moderate activity improves one's well-being and strength. It also seems to help prevent bladder problems and constipation. Make sure you have help getting up at first, though. Every day, try to do a few more things. However, don't push yourself if you feel weak or feverish. Movement keeps the

After the Baby Is Born

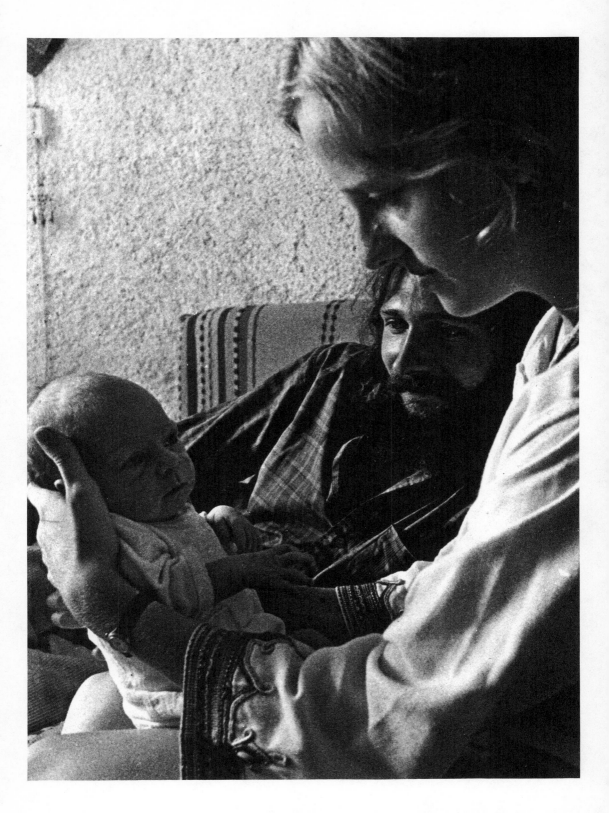

muscles in tone and improves circulation. Good circulation is important in avoiding phlebitis. If you must remain in bed, your doctor may suggest some exercises that can be done in bed to aid muscle tone and circulation. Some doctors may prescribe massages. Normal activity probably won't be resumed for a month or so. Keeping track of temperature and pulse are an effective way of spotting postpartum complications.

Following labor it is normal to experience a vaginal discharge composed of blood, mucus, and other substances from the uterus. This discharge is called lochia. The flow during the days immediately after labor is the heaviest. It will diminish between the eighth and the fifteenth day. The odor of the flow is similar to that of the menstrual flow. Two or three external washings with a jet of sterile water are recommended. Bandages and sanitary napkins should be changed as often as necessary. If the mother has had stitches, the dressings should be dry. They are usually not necessary after the fifth or sixth day. Injections are usually not necessary.

Constipation is often a problem after delivery. Elimination can be painful, especially if an episiotomy has been performed. A mild laxative can help this situation. It is important not to put too much stress on this area to aid healing. Washing after elimination is a good idea. Any problems that may develop can be cleared up easily with simple medications.

Generally there are no restrictions on food at this point. If you are nursing, make sure that your food intake is substantial and avoid foods that cause gas (garlic, cabbage, and asparagus, for example). These foods will give the milk an unsavory flavor and may cause digestive problems for the child. Drink a lot of fluids. Avoid alcohol and smoking, especially around the child.

Sexual relations are not advised until after the postpartum visit to the doctor. It is important to make sure that everything has healed properly. Bleeding and fever can result from resuming intercourse too soon.

POTENTIAL PROBLEMS
IN THE POSTPARTUM PHASE

It is normal for body temperature to go up to about 100.4 when milk production begins. Any other fevers are most often the result of infection and must be observed carefully. The infection can be of internal or external origin. An infection of the lymphatic channels of the breast may develop around the seventh day. This is marked by a sudden elevation in body temperature (between 101° and 102° F) and by pain and redness in the breasts. Each case of infection must be considered separately. Modern cleansing techniques have cut down on infections tremendously.

Often, elevations in temperature and pulse follow one another. However, in cases of phlebitis the temperature rises and pulse rates drop.

Bleeding may develop in the postpartum phase. Around the tenth day you may notice a flow of blood. The flow comes on rapidly and leaves just as rapidly. This is a "mini-period" and shows that the lining of the uterus is restoring itself. If there is a hormonal imbalance or a lack of elasticity in the uterine muscle, the flow may last longer. New mothers may think that some part of the afterbirth is still in the uterus, but this is unlikely. Check with your doctor if you feel uncertain about any bleeding. The postpartum phase is a time to be alert to any abnormalities in the healing process. The menstrual cycle usually returns without incident.

Other Postpartum Considerations

Even if you feel quite good physically, you should avoid fatigue. Don't overdo it in your work or in visits to friends and relatives. If you are nursing, you may lose weight more slowly than if you are not nursing. If you are concerned about your weight, find your target weight on one of the many weight charts available. To lose weight, avoid excessive starches, sugars, and salt. Begin an exercise program to restore your muscle tone. We have included one below.

Do not take any medications without consulting your doctor. Many things are going on in your body, and you don't want to disturb them.

PHYSICAL EXERCISES FOR THE POSTPARTUM PERIOD

During your pregnancy, your body had to modify itself in many ways. Many muscles are now soft and distended, particularly the abdominal muscles. These following exercises will help you regain muscle tone. The conditions under which each person exercises vary. If you like you can do them at home. If you don't like exercising alone, you may want to do it with friends. If your pregnancy and delivery were difficult or if you had a cesarean, you may need special exercises.

These exercises are designed to aid different areas of the body. They will strengthen the abdominal muscles and the muscles along the spinal column, improve blood circulation, and improve the muscles around the perineum. You should check with your doctor before beginning any exercise program.

The Abdominal Muscles

Below are two exercises designed to strengthen the abdominal muscles.

1. Lie flat on the floor, and hook your feet under a bed or heavy chair (Fig. 1). With your arms by your side, sit up without the aid of your arms (Fig. 2).
Repeat these sit-ups three times each day, increasing daily the number of times you do them. If you find it difficult to sit up vertically in the beginning, sit up as far as you can three times daily until you strengthen yourself enough to do full sit-ups.
2. Lie down on the floor, and stretch out your arms. Straighten out your legs and try to touch your left hand with your right foot (Fig. 3). After doing this, return to the starting position, and try to touch your right hand with your left foot. Start by doing this exercise five times daily, increasing the number as you are able.

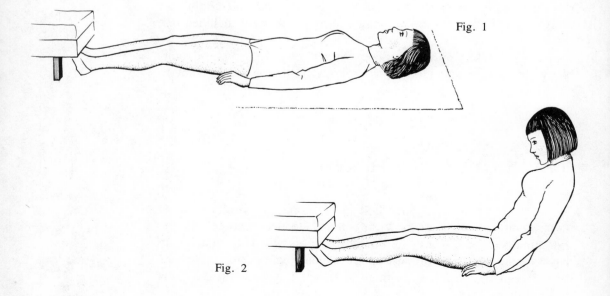

Fig. 1

Fig. 2

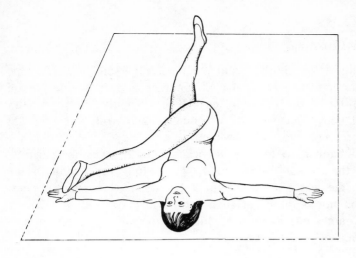

Fig. 3

The Muscles of the Back

1. Sit on the floor, with your legs apart. Stretch out your arms, and touch your right foot with your left hand (Fig. 4). Return to the starting position, and touch your left foot with your right hand. If you don't want to sit on the floor, you can do this exercise standing up. Repeat this exercise five times on each side, increasing the number as you are able.

2. Stand with your back to the wall, with your heels, buttocks, shoulders, and back of the head touching the wall (Fig. 5). Inhale deeply, while holding in the stomach muscles, until the small of the back presses against the wall (Fig. 6). Repeat this exercise about 10 times daily.

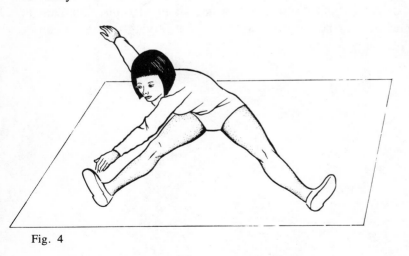

Fig. 4

Fig. 5   Fig. 6

Blood Circulation

Walking is the simplest and most natural exercise. Each time you take a step, the leg muscles contract and make the blood circulate in the veins of your legs. It is difficult to recommend precise distances, but we do recommend that you walk on flat terrain and do not overexert yourself.

If you happen to be on the beach and the weather permits, walking in the ocean is very good. Walk along the length of the beach, with the water level at your knees. (It is, however, imperative that you not be alone at such a time.)

Below are some exercises which aid circulation that you can do in the house.

1. Lie on your back and extend your legs. Supporting your back with your arms (Fig. 7), raise your trunk and legs vertically off the floor. Move your feet in a pedaling motion for a few minutes. If, in the beginning, you have trouble rotating your legs in the vertical position, lie on your back and rotate your legs (Fig. 8).
2. Stand with arms extended and place your hands on a piece of furniture (Fig. 9). Rise up on the balls of your feet, and hold your position for a count of three. Do this exercise 10 times a day in the beginning, and increase as you are able.

Muscles of the Perineum

This exercise is very important. You may want to check with your doctor to make sure that you are doing it right. Contract the muscles of your pelvic floor, as if you were trying to stop urination.

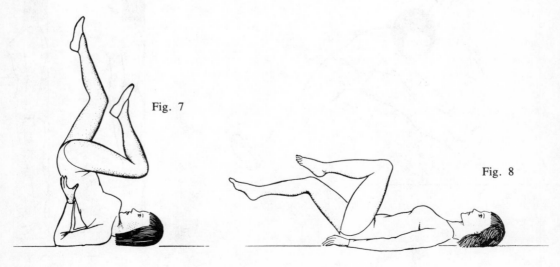

Fig. 7

Fig. 8

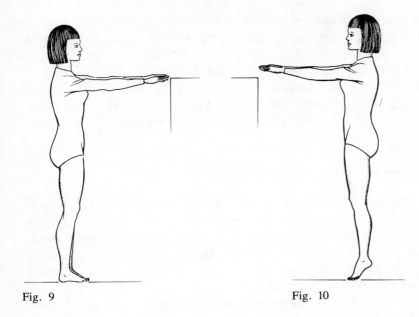

Fig. 9   Fig. 10

Keep pulling these muscles in until they are quite tight. Then release them slowly. Do this several times a day, if possible.

If possible, do all of these exercises during three or four sessions a day. Their effect will be felt more quickly then, and you will regain your general body tone rapidly.

POSTNATAL CONSULTATION

The postnatal consultation is very important. Many women feel that it is not necessary if everything is going normally. It is important to verify that your general physical condition is good, to take your blood pressure, and to make sure that involution of the uterus is complete. The doctor will also check for details that can escape your notice. The cervical canal or uterus could be mildly infected, or the uterus may not have returned to its original position.

POSTPARTUM DEPRESSION

Depression is a problem for many new mothers. Often it comes on a person suddenly and leaves after a few hours. Sometimes these feelings of depression are more prolonged. The mother wakes up tired, and small tasks seen insurmountable. She may feel deserted by her husband and family. Interacting with them may seem like a burden. She may feel like crying for no apparent reason.

Many mothers experience these feelings. It is important to know that they may happen to you, so that you will not be alarmed if you feel depressed from time to time. If you experience these emotions, consider them calmly and be assured that they will pass.

Causes of Postpartum Depression

During pregnancy, especially during the first and last trimesters, women may experience vague feelings of depression which may be provoked by frustrations or difficulties in adapting themselves to a new role. These feelings may extend into the first week after childbirth (especially when milk begins to flow) or occur around the tenth or fifteenth day at home.

Several theories have been advanced as to why this occurs. Hormone levels are in a state of flux, and you are not yet up to par physically. You are also adjusting to a new role, and this can be very demanding. We will go over the possible causes of these feelings, to enable you to deal with them, should they occur.

Adaptation to the new role is easier if the pregnancy was desired and happened under good conditions. However, this is not always the case. Perhaps the pregnancy was accepted more than desired, and the new mother may have unresolved feelings about the whole event.

Anxiety can show itself in many ways. Fatigue, depression, and a morose attitude can make one more susceptible to anxiety. Ambivalence frequently accompanies the experience of having a child. People often have doubts about the pregnancy, but they are still happy about it. Depression does not happen to everyone. Speaking with your doctor and family if it does occur can help you express your feelings and gain their support during this important time.

After childbirth, the woman may feel disoriented. Many diverse tensions have accumulated during the last months, both mental and physical. A sense of emptiness may be felt. Childbirth itself is a tiring experience, and she needs to recover physically from this. Uterine problems can cause digestive difficulties. The sudden emptying of the uterus also must be adjusted to.

Advice for the New Mother

If you experience postpartum depression, you should not try to ignore it. Instead, you should acknowledge what is happening and try to minimize the effects.

Before the baby arrives, your house should be organized and prepared for the baby's routine as much as possible. This will make your daily routine much easier when you return from the hospital. Keep important telephone numbers close at hand. This may help alleviate any unconscious fear you may be experiencing. Your feelings are *not* due to any personal inadequacy. Talk to the people around you (medical personnel and family) if fears and depressed feelings are bothering you.

CONTRACEPTION

After childbirth you may think, "I would like to have another child, but not right away. What should I do?" Contraception permits you to space your children in the manner that best suits you. Modern methods of contraception can be divided into three general categories: periodic abstinence, local contraceptives, and oral contraceptives.

Periodic Abstinence

The method of contraception using periodic abstinence is commonly known as the rhythm method or natural family planning. It is based on the fact that women usually ovulate between the twelfth and sixteenth days of their monthly period. Using these figures, one can calculate that the period of fertility is from the seventh day after the last period to 12 days before the next. However, many women do not have regular cycles, and sometimes ovulation does not happen on schedule. So the method of relying only on numerical estimates is not reliable. Fortunately, there is a more precise method of fixing the date of ovulation, by keeping track of changes in body temperature.

To use this method, a woman must keep a daily record of her body temperature, taken at the same time of day, every day, for a month or two. She will notice that her temperature after a menstrual period is somewhat lower than after ovulation, when it will rise between about 0.6 and 0.8° F. A short dip in body temperature occurs before ovulation. It is important that each person keep track of her own temperatures since there is much individual variation in this matter. Therefore, when a woman notices a small dip followed by a sharp rise in temperature, she knows that ovulation has taken place. She should then refrain from intercourse for four days. The time of greatest security is from the fourth day after ovulation till the beginning of the next period. The time preceding ovulation is not as secure, because a cycle might be cut short or a person might have an irregular cycle. If you have an irregular cycle, it is possible to find the time of relative safety by studying the length of your cycles. If your shortest cycle is 19 days and your longest cycle is 26 days, subtract 19 from 26 to get 7. The first 7 days of your cycle are the time of relative safety. This method is quite effective if a woman has a regular cycle and takes her temperature faithfully. It is ineffective if the woman does not take and record her temperature regularly and accurately.

It is also important to remember that aspects of life other than one's menstrual cycle can affect body temperature, such as activity level, weather, clothing, and one's state of health.

Localized Contraception

Localized contraception is a type of barrier in either the vagina or uterus or over the penis. Vaginal barriers are designed to stop the sperm from entering the cervical canal. The most popular device of this type is the diaphragm, a circular piece of rubber designed to cover the cervix. It must fit the diameter of the cervix. For this reason it is necessary that individuals be fitted for the correct size. Also, it must be (1) placed in the vagina for each act of intercourse, (2) covered with a spermicidal cream or jelly before being placed in the vagina and before each act of intercourse that occurs while the diaphragm is still in place, and (3) removed no fewer than 6 to 8 hours after intercourse. Diaphragms used with spermicides are about 96% effective, but some people don't like them because of the advance preparations necessary.

Intrauterine devices (IUDs) are plastic/metal forms that are placed in the uterus by a doctor. They can be left in place for 1 to 3 years or indefinitely and are impervious to X-rays. They cannot be used if any form of infection is present. They have several advantages over other methods of contraception: (1) They are effective. (2) The woman is not usually aware of the presence of the device, and she does not have to do anything. (3) They are also good for women who cannot take oral contraceptives or who forget to take them regularly.

Intrauterine devices also have serious drawbacks, as well, and these should be considered very carefully before making a decision to have one inserted. IUDs are commonly associated with increased blood loss during, and sometimes between, menstrual periods as well as with abdominal pain. Women who do not have infection when an IUD is inserted experience an increase in the risk of subsequent pelvic inflammatory disease of about three times (300%) what it is for women without an IUD.

People with previous experiences with pelvic infection, multiple sex partners, and those under the age of 25 who have never had children run a higher risk of complications than others. In addition, IUDs do not protect against ectopic pregnancies (those that occur outside the uterus—e.g., tubal and cornual pregnancies).

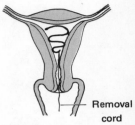

One type of intrauterine device (Lippes Loop) in place.

Less effective methods of local contraception include condoms (for men), foams, jellies, and suppositories.

Oral Contraceptives

Oral contraceptives (the Pill) are 99% effective. They work by blocking ovulation, and for this reason they can be used as a treatment for various gynecological problems. Pills combine various combinations of the hormones estrogen and progesterone. Some combine both estrogens and progesterones in each pill.

Some brands consist of 28 pills; 21 contain active ingredients; the remaining have no active ingredients. This is to help women to remember to take a pill daily. Other packets contain 21. After taking a pill for each day, no pills are taken for 7 days. You begin taking the pill on the fifth day of your cycle, the first day being the beginning of your period. After pregnancy, pills are taken again after the first period. If the patient desires a method of contraception before the resumption of menstruation, it is possible to take the pill 10 days after delivery. Protection is not assured during the first menstrual cycle, but it is complete in the following cycles.

Oral contraceptives can be obtained only with a doctor's prescription. They are potent drugs that affect the entire system. A complete physical examination is necessary. Weight, blood pressure, and blood tests must be taken. Oral contraceptives are contraindicated for women with phlebitis or hypertension. People with a family history of diabetes or breast or endometrial cancer, those who are obese, and those over 35 years of age might do well to consider another form of contraception. It is advised that people who smoke cigarettes *not* use oral contraceptives. Each instance must be considered individually by the doctor and patient.

For oral contraceptives to be effective, you must take them daily. Missing even one will lessen their effectiveness. Most of the packets have the days of the week written on them to help you remember to take them. If you forget to take one at night, take it the following day. If you forget to resume taking them after a period, use an alternative method of contraception for that month, then begin taking them on the fifth day of your following cycle. If you stop taking the pills, ovulation starts again, and you can become pregnant. If you wish to become pregnant, it is recommended that you wait an interval of three months between stopping the pill and becoming pregnant.

STERILIZATION

You may decide that you have had all the children you want, and you may choose permanent contraception, or sterilization. One of the most popular methods of accomplishing this is the laparoscopic tubal ligation. Two small incisions are made, one on either side of the lower abdominal region. Through these incisions, the Fallopian tubes are grasped with surgical instruments and cut and/or burned electrically to prevent the passage of any more eggs from the ovaries through the Fallopian tubes into the uterus.

You should discuss the particulars of this surgery in detail with your physician. Although in rare instances the procedure can be reversed to permit a subsequent pregnancy, tubal ligation is considered permanent and should not be undertaken if you feel you might want to have another child.

There are inherent risks in laparoscopic tubal ligation, as there are in all surgical procedures. They should be investigated and discussed fully with your physician and considered seriously before you make any final choice. If you do decide to have a tubal ligation (sometimes referred to as "having one's tubes tied"), investigate your surgeon's experience in this particular procedure. How long has he or she been performing this procedure, and how many tubal ligations has your doctor done? Make sure you are satisfied that you have been fully informed on all the particulars; you have a right to ask, and you have a right to know.

9

LEAVING THE HOSPITAL

In cases in which the birth proceeded normally, birth weight of the infant is sufficient, and there are no postpartum complications, you will probably leave the hospital on the fourth day. During this time, you should be fairly well rested and beginning to feel better. You have probably learned many things about your baby and are now ready to assume your new role. If there were any complications with any aspect of the birth process, a longer stay may be required. Your doctor will decide when you can go home safely.

THE BABY FINDS
HIS OR HER RHYTHM

The baby's day is made up of periods of sleep, followed by periods of eating and wakefulness. Acquiring this rhythm is a somewhat mysterious process, although medical science does know part of the process. Some factors are quite obvious, and we will examine these.

Life Rhythm before Birth

The rhythm of the fetus is largely determined by the mother's daily rhythm. Arrival of food and oxygen parallels the mother's intake of food and oxygen. Periods of rest and activity also reflect the mother's schedule. It seems that the fetus rests when the mother is active and becomes active when the mother is trying to sleep. When the mother is active, the fetus is rocked in the amniotic fluid. This rocking stops when the mother sits or lies down. The fetus also is

Returning Home

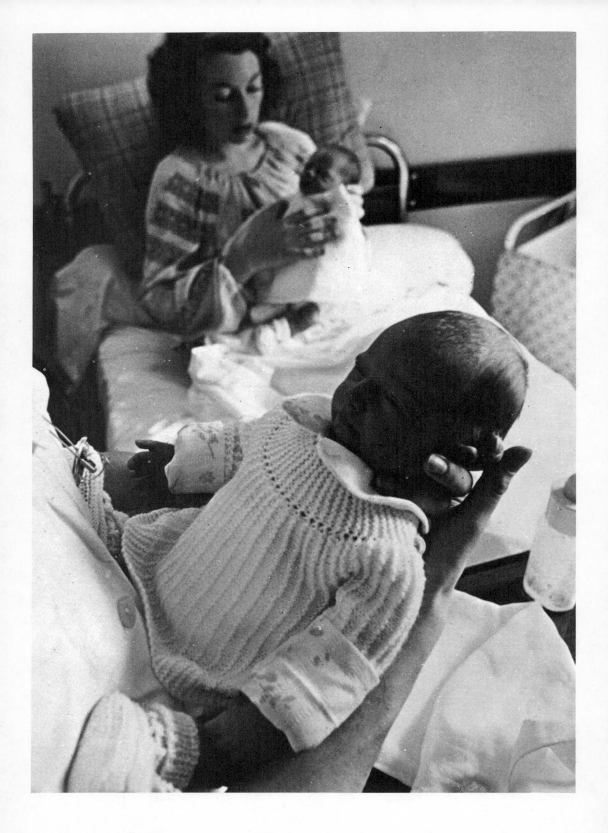

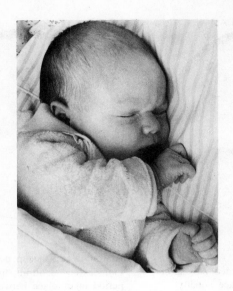

aware of the maternal heartbeat. This heart beats at a rate of 70 to 80 beats per minute, and this is the rate that babies find the most soothing.

After Birth

A combination of fetal rhythm and the circumstances of life shape the infant's own rhythm. These circumstances include: succession of day and night, temperature of the room, and availability of the mother. Factors of physiology and nourishment are also important. These include the ability to maintain a reserve of energy, the capacity for absorption of food, and the rate of digestion of food.

Energy is needed for many things, such as growth, cellular exchanges, and a strong cardiac rhythm. Because the infant is limited in ability to absorb food and has few energy reserves, he or she must eat frequently (about every 3 hours). In the following months, energy needs will diminish as reserves are built up. Reserves will begin to accumulate under the skin, in the muscle tissue, and in the liver. Capacities for absorbing nourishment will also increase, and meals will become less frequent.

During the first week of life, the newborn is no longer subject to mother's rhythm but has still not established his or her own. The baby is not yet influenced by the differences in light and noise that mark day and night. By the end of the second or third week, moments of wakefulness tend to concentrate in three periods daily of about 1 hour each. These usually occur in the morning, afternoon,

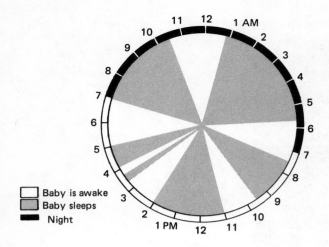
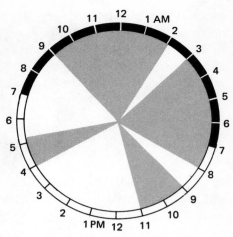

☐ Baby is awake	
▨ Baby sleeps	
■ Night	

Daily sleep rhythm. At two weeks, sleep is divided into short periods that take place equally over a 24-hour period. The baby does not yet distinguish between day and night.

At four weeks, sleep periods become more extended during the night. A long period takes place between 9 P.M. and 2 A.M. The baby wakes up for an hour between 2 and 3 A.M. and sleeps from 3 to 8 A.M. During the day, the baby sleeps for two short periods, from 9 to 11 A.M. and from 4 to 5 P.M. The baby is starting to distinguish between day and night.

and night and do not coincide with feeding times. By the fourth or sixth week, these periods of wakefulness divide into two periods, one in the morning and one at night.

Activities during periods of wakefulness vary from child to child and depend on a number of factors. The two major ones are the amount of energy the child needs to expend, and the ability he or she has to communicate with the exterior world. Muscular activity (sucking on the fist, crying, and moving the extremities and head) account for some of the activity. Activities that relate to the outside world vary with maturity and age. These activities include following objects visually, interest in objects he or she can see, and reaction to sounds. The senses are somewhat underdeveloped at this time. The most important tactile stimuli are sucking and being held in your arms. As with adults, each child's response to stimuli varies. Some need a lot of activity; others are calmer.

Calm babies suck on their fingers for long periods of time and sleep a lot. More active ones wake up easily at the slightest noise, cry a lot, and wave their arms and legs. Each child makes contact with the exterior world in a different way. It is possible to draw some conclusions on infant behavior. Children who eat slowly and

suck on their fingers a lot cry less than those who eat quickly and
don't suck on their fingers as much. As the child's ability to relate
to the outside world grows and as the child learns to suck on fingers
and be entertained through the developing senses, the need to cry to
release energy lessens.

CRYING

Crying is the only way that your baby has to express him- or herself. Apart from sucking, it is also the only form of exercise the
newborn can do. The young mother must learn how to understand
this language. Tears usually can have several different meanings.
They can mean that the baby is tired, is in pain, or is experiencing
discomfort.

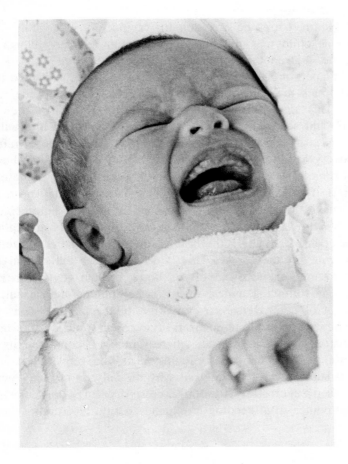

It is easy to tell if the child is tired or hungry. If the crying begins before a scheduled feeding, it may be that the milk from the last feeding was not enough to satisfy the child's growing needs for food. Experiment with increasing the amount slightly if the baby wakes up before scheduled feedings quite often. Experience will teach you when the baby is crying because of hunger.

If the baby starts crying suddenly and with force, it may be that he or she is experiencing pain or discomfort. Check to make sure that diaper pins are properly fastened. Then check to see if there is anything in the crib or blankets that is irritating the child. If you have other children, they may have put something in the crib they thought the baby might like that is annoying the infant. During the first three months colic is a frequent cause of tears. This begins around the end of the fourth week. It is often most severe after the evening feeding and in active, vigorous babies. Colic affects boys more often than girls. This subject is covered more extensively in the section titled "Colic."

Discomfort may be a reason for crying. As with adults, what annoys one child may not bother another one. Damp diapers may bother one, and another won't cry though the diapers are very wet. If dirty diapers are the problem, it is easy enough to change them.

At times the baby may simply need to dissipate some excess energy. This may occur at times when the child has been fed, changed, and seems to have no reason to cry. He or she will cry loudly and wave arms and legs vigorously. The bottle is refused, and the crying doesn't stop even when you pick him or her up. Several minutes later the baby stops crying as suddenly as he or she started. If it seems to you that this is the case, it may be a good idea to leave the child in the crib for a few minutes before picking him or her up. If your baby drinks a bottle vigorously and quickly, you may consider making the hole of the bottle smaller, or tightening the ring on the bottle. This way, the child will spend more energy getting the milk out of the bottle, and have less to spend crying. The following nap should also be sounder than usual.

A lot of controversy surrounds use of the pacifier. It is often effective in stopping children from crying, but some doctors do not think that it is a good device, whereas others recommend its use. You must decide under what circumstances you want to use it and not let it substitute for finding out why the baby is crying. Pacifiers can be used successfully to stop excessive crying, particularly the kind that comes from needing to expend energy. Use during the first

3 or 4 months is perfectly acceptable, and may prevent a child from developing a thumb-sucking habit. After 3 or 4 months of age, try to avoid using the pacifier to calm the baby.

Sometimes the baby cries because he or she wants your attention. This crying is easy to recognize. It happens at irregular times, and the baby stops crying when you pick him or her up or talk softly. The method of dealing with this type of crying varies from person to person. Some mothers think that the baby should not be crying unless there is an obvious reason, such as hunger or wet diapers. So when the baby cries for no apparent reason, they just let the baby cry. They may not think that it is possible for such a small baby to feel lonely. This approach is effective if one judges success by weight gain alone. Mothers who overly systematize childcare, and who may not be totally at ease with the affection element of mothering, are prone to take this attitude. Their babies are clean and well cared for, but may long for affection and attention. Admittedly, this is an extreme situation, but attitudes like this can be very damaging to the child's development.

Other mothers practice another style of childcare that may appear extreme. They jump to the child's side at every cry or sound. They spend a lot of time rocking and talking to the baby. These conversations often seem incomprehensible to people around the mother and child. They may neglect activities that they formerly considered very important. A great bond between mother and child is being developed by all of this attention.

One observes a slower rate of development when children are hospitalized for long periods of time or are routinely left in crowded day-care centers where there is not sufficient personnel to give the attention that the child needs. Children in this situation often develop a gloomy outlook on life and do not appear happy to the casual observer. They do not grow psychologically or physically and may even lose ground in these areas. When they are returned to a traditional environment, a more normal rate of growth returns.

Two extremes of mothering have been described above. Probably your own style will depend on your circumstances and personality. We offer these extremes as food for thought. In this way you can consider how you can best raise your child. When your thoughts on your own approach to motherhood are clear, you will not be subject to every well-intentioned suggestion that comes your way. It is critical that the mother-child relationship be based on the way *you* want to raise your child.

WHEN MUST YOU CHANGE THE BABY?

The baby should be changed whenever the diapers are soiled. During the first 6 weeks, the baby will cry when the diapers are dirty. Check the condition of the diapers each time the baby cries. After a few days, you will become adept at the process.

Very often the baby will move his or her bowels while eating, because the act of eating moves other things along in the digestive tract. The baby stops sucking and may begin crying. When he or she is finished, the feeding continues. Or the baby may empty the bowels soon after the feeding.

BATHING THE BABY

The bath is an important moment in the baby's day. You can use a cotton washcloth and a mild soap, which is much better for the baby than other varieties of soap.

You can bathe the baby in a plastic bath designed for the purpose, or you can use the sink until he or she becomes too big for it. This usually happens at about 3 months. If you are using the sink, be very, very careful that the baby does not fall against the faucets or any other hazardous parts in the sink.

Before putting the baby in the tub, make sure that the water temperature throughout is comfortable to the touch. You should try to bathe the baby in a warm room so that he or she doesn't become chilled when taken out of the tub.

Finding a good time to bathe the baby may require some experimentation. You should find a time that is quiet and free from interruptions. The morning is as good as the afternoon, depending on your schedule. Do not bathe the baby immediately before feeding time. He or she will undoubtedly be very cranky and will probably fall back to sleep from exhaustion without having eaten. Bathing the baby right after a feeding is also not a good idea, because the extra activity may cause digestive problems and probably will result in burping up the last feeding. Waiting for ½ hour after the feeding and then giving the bath may well be a good procedure. Digestion is well under way, and the baby is probably relaxed at this time. Or, if this does not prove to be a good time, you can try waking the baby up about ¾ of an hour before the scheduled feeding. By the time feeding time rolls around, the baby will be clean and dry.

Babies should be bathed daily if they are in good health. This is necessary because they are often soiled from a variety of causes during the course of a day. Bathing is the best way to avoid skin problems. The only exceptions to this rule take place when the baby has particularly sensitive skin or if your water is particularly hard. Your doctor will advise you in these cases.

To avoid confusion, you should prepare for the baby's bath ahead of time. A clean towel, washcloth, and change of clothes should be close at hand. Turn up your sleeves, and remove any jewelry or rings that might scratch the baby. Wash your hands carefully with soap. Put your elbow in the water to check the water temperature. It should be about body temperature. Make sure that the faucet is cool and that the hot water is securely turned off.

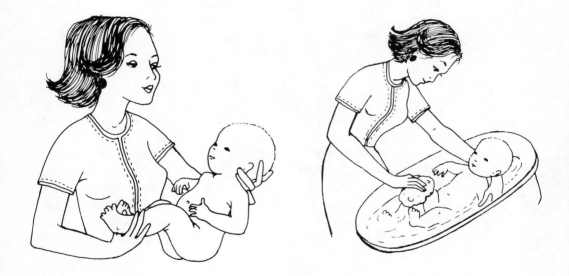

Lather up the washcloth. Wash the baby while he or she is lying on a clean towel on the counter. Be sure to wash all of the folds in the skin, paying particular attention to the thighs, armpits, and neck. Then rinse the baby in the sink or tub. Be very careful how you hold the baby, because the soap will make the skin slippery. To make sure that the baby doesn't slip out of your hands, hold the baby's ankles with your left hand (with your right hand if you are left-handed), and place your right hand under the child's neck while supporting the head with the thumb and index finger. Keep the head above ear level in the water. The baby will be half seated in the water, with back and head supported by your left hand. After rinsing the soap off, dry with a clean towel.

You may be tempted to clean out the ear canal with a cotton swab. Do not do this. If the outer ear needs to be cleaned, you may use a moist washcloth wrapped around one of your fingers. The ear canal has its own cleaning system. Tiny hairs line it, and move excess waste from the interior of the ear to the outer portion. The use of cotton swabs interferes with this process, and blockages of wax result. Cotton swabs can also injure the eardrum.

Do not use cotton swabs on the nasal passages either. The baby will sneeze from time to time, and this is sufficient to clear the passages. If the air in your home is hot and dry, mucus may dry around the edges of the nostrils and form small pieces of hard mucus. Don't try to pull these off. Soften them first by putting a small amount of oil around the nasal area without getting it into the nasal passages. They will soften and be pushed out by sneezing. If they are very superficial, you can gently remove them with a cotton swab.

It is not necessary to wash the hair daily; two or three times a week is sufficient. Use the same soap that you use for the baby's bath.

During the first weeks you must pay particular attention to the navel area. After the cord has fallen off, you may notice a red scab forming from time to time. This is no cause for alarm. Your doctor will probably have specific instructions for navel care.

It is customary to cover the baby's bottom with cream and baby powder after each change. These creams are generally made up of a zinc oxide base that protects the skin from the humidity of the diapers and helps to prevent diaper rash. Many brand names exist, and your doctor may advise you on which one to use. Different types of baby powders exist, but the utility of this product is limited.

Bath oils are used by some to make the baby smell nice. The utility of these products is very limited. They should not be used on the face, because the skin of a newborn infant already has a lot of oil in it. Some babies even have acnelike formations on their faces. It is also useless for the rest of the body. The only area that may be helped by these products is the bottom. Your doctor may suggest oils if this area is too dry.

Several remarks should be made regarding the best way to clean the genital areas of infants. In baby girls a few drops of blood may be passed during the first days. This is normal and no cause for alarm. During the bath or at changing time, you should clean the vulva thoroughly to make sure that no urine or fecal matter remains. Proceed gently from the front to the back. Wrap a compress around your finger. Use soap for the cleansing of this area. Separate the external lips of the vulva and clean in the folds; then separate and clean the interior lips. Next clean the anal area. Then rinse the genital area in the same manner, proceeding from front to back.

In baby boys, wash gently, as with the rest of the body. If your son has not been circumcised, you must release the foreskin from the penile glans. Proceed slowly and gently. Try to loosen the foreskin, and push it back over the penis. At first this will seem difficult, because the two surfaces are not entirely separate. As the foreskin is released, you will find a whitish, strongly odorous substance underneath. This substance is called smegma. You can remove it with a clean compress.

Sometimes there is a narrow opening in the foreskin that does not permit it to be pushed over the penis. If this is the case, do not try to dilate the opening and push the foreskin back. If you do this, you risk blocking the foreskin behind the glans, you will stop blood circulation in the glans, and surgical intervention will have to take place immediately. If you are uncertain as to how to go about this matter, speak with your physician.

DRESSING THE BABY

The bath has been finished, the baby is dry, and now you must dress him or her. At first, this may seem like a long, sometimes frustrating experience. With practice, everything will become easier. See Chapter 3 for wardrobe suggestions.

Put on the cotton undershirt and snap it shut. Next put on a tee shirt, sweater, or other outer garment. Many mothers use stretch suits during the first few months. If you want to save time, try sliding the undershirt into the overgarment. If time is very short, you can skip the undershirt, and simply put the tee shirt on. Diaper the baby, and tuck the shirts into the diaper.

The season and temperature are important considerations in dressing the baby. The temperature of your home should also be considered. You will probably overdress your baby. An undershirt, tee shirt, followed by several sweaters seem to be fairly standard indoor clothing during the winter months. Use your own comfort as a way of deciding what the baby should wear. If you are comfortable with one layer of clothing, the baby should also be dressed lightly. If you feel chilly, the baby needs more clothing. If your home is poorly heated, obviously you must dress the baby warmly.

Often an undershirt and a tee shirt are sufficient. During warm weather, this tendency to overdress the baby is dangerous. Wool blankets are too heavy above 85° F; cotton blankets will suffice at these temperatures. During extremely hot days, or if your home is exposed to the midday sun, the temperature can reach 90° F or more. Do not hesitate to leave the baby in a light shirt and without a blanket on such days.

10

FOR FATHERS

In discussions of child development, the role of the mother is assumed to be central to the child's personality growth. The role of the father is usually acknowledged as being very important, but has often been overlooked in all further discussions. Fathers have been portrayed as remote from day-to-day family life, and as concerned mainly with discipline and setting a good example for the children.

Such a wide division of child-rearing responsibilities can make husband and wife feel that something is dramatically wrong. Wives feel overburdened by the multitudinous tasks that come with having a newborn (the difficulty of getting adequate sleep in between night feedings, for example), and fathers recognize that they have a responsibility, but may not be sure where it lies. If he misses all of the day-to-day tasks, he also misses a lot of the child's growth.

This strict division of responsibility is becoming rarer in our culture. Women take their place in the world, and the world is becoming richer for it. Men are finding their place in the family, and families are benefitting tremendously as a result. This is not always easy, and for this reason we would now like to speak directly to the fathers.

It may seem that this book was written mainly for mothers. We have explained the development of her pregnancy to prepare her for each step of the way. For you, the coming of a child has not affected your daily life in a radical fashion. You have probably noticed that your wife may have had problems with nausea, and certainly you were excited when you heard that she was pregnant,

Baby Finds a Place in the Family

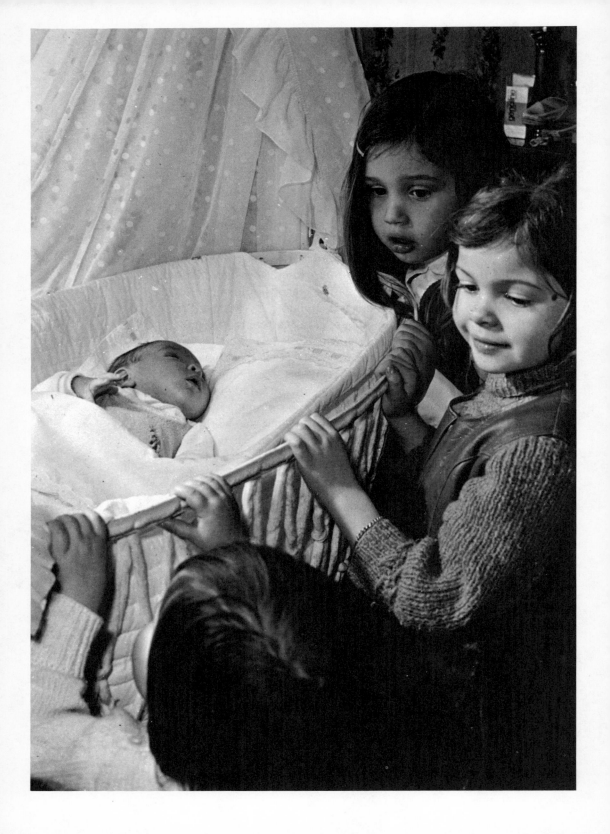

but little has changed in your daily life. The baby seemed a distant reality, one that may not have occupied your thoughts too much.

The situation is different for your wife. The pregnancy means that a drastic change has taken place. Physical and emotional adjustments will have to be dealt with. Some of these adjustments will be large, and some will be small. You may not even be aware of many of them. Her sleep patterns will be different; you may notice that she tosses and turns more as she sleeps. Her reactions to different situations may be different than previously. Problems of work and social affairs may be secondary to her at this time. Don't be annoyed with her if her reactions to you are different. She will probably want to talk about the pregnancy. Listen to her, and try to support her during this time. Remember that you are *both* responsible for the pregnancy.

Ask your wife if she wants you to accompany her to the doctor. Some women prefer going alone, others like their husband to go also. Help her with any administrative problems that are taken care of at the doctor's office.

After a few months, your wife's figure will begin to change. This may disturb her a bit, and she needs your assurance that you still find her womanly and attractive. Her attitudes toward sex may change. She will become tired more easily and should *not* have to be solely responsible for the household chores. Don't let her do heavy work, and help her with lifting objects that need to be moved or carried. Getting the baby's room in order is a project in which both father and mother should participate. Consider her desires and needs during this time of change.

Childbirth and the Postnatal Period

Your wife may ask you to participate in natural childbirth classes. Our experience has been that husbands make excellent assistants by helping their wives with breathing and timing the contractions. The decision rests with you and your wife. You should make sure that you discuss it thoroughly and honestly before arriving at a decision. Some psychologists think that it is important for the father to be in the labor room. All of this is speculative, and it is up to each couple and the medical staff to determine what is best in a given situation.

Most of the drastic changes in your life will begin after the baby has been born. In the midst of your delight in your new child, you will find that your life has become more hectic. Your family's day-to-day routine is centered around the baby. Meals may not be on time, and the food may be different, because if your wife is nursing, she has to be careful of what she eats. She'll be avoiding some types of foods because they affect the milk adversely. You may feel distant from your wife during this time because she has to spend so much time and concern on the baby.

Consider the return of your wife from the hospital. Try to make it a special and relaxing time. Above all, make sure that the house is in good order. Allowing your wife to come home to a dirty house and piles of laundry is irresponsible and inconsiderate. The last week has been an exhausting one for her, and she has a right to your help in getting back to normal.

Returning Home

When mother and child return home from the hospital, you'll begin to notice a change in your day-to-day routine. You may feel burdened at times by your new responsibilities, and your wife may seem overwhelmed and discouraged by the matters at hand. You should try to provide a stabilizing element to the situation. Try to be encouraging and calm. If you notice that you are anxious, rest assured that this is a normal feeling and that it will pass.

A sense of frustration may creep in. Your sleep is disturbed, your leisure time is not as flexible as previously, and you must figure out a way to budget in the baby financially. All of this is to be expected, but it can be disturbing just the same. On top of this, you and your wife don't have as much time together as you formerly shared. It is very important to approach all of this positively, and not to retreat in silence from the situation. It is important for you to let your wife know what you are thinking, and for the two of you to communicate regularly on how each is handling the new circumstances. By doing this, you will have support from one another, and then will be better able to handle things. Your wife will undoubtedly have a lot to share with you, too, and will respect and appreciate your openness.

Try not to feel clumsy when dressing or feeding the baby. Do your share in providing the night feedings. All of these things build relationships between you, your wife, and your child. A triangular relationship will develop, and this ties the family together. Disruptions in this triangle affect each person involved.

You may find this aspect of family relations surprising. You may have thought that it was too early to speak of your role. Even in this book we have dealt largely with the mother's role. Writing a separate section for fathers may seem to imply an artificial differ-

entiation between the roles. Although the roles are often broken down into functional categories for practicality's sake, the family itself forms a complete unit. As husband and father you are tremendously important to the child's life.

There are many different kinds of families. The character of the family determines how the children will be raised. It is dangerous to generalize about family situations, because they vary so much. Nevertheless, we will consider some of the basic structures of family life.

The mother is central to the baby's life during the first months after birth. By being born, the child has taken the first step toward differentiating itself from mother. This does not mean that the father does not play an important role in the child's life during this time. The mother may be the infant's primary contact with the outside world. But the father also exerts a great deal of influence on the child's environment. His attitude is reflected from mother to child. If the father is supportive and cooperative, the child will benefit for many reasons. You can easily see that a child will grow up more peacefully if his or her mother is optimistic and happy and if the child has pleasant interactions with the father. By supporting your child's mother and participating in the child's day-to-day routine, you exert tremendous influence on your son's or daughter's world.

In the coming months, as the baby learns to recognize different faces, the father broadens the child's perception and experience. The mother may represent the familiar world of the home, and the father often brings the outside world to the child. The child slowly begins to know of the world of adults and that of children.

In a certain sense, the father is the first stranger in the child's life. After the shock of finding out that the mother does not exist for the child alone, the child begins to learn about human relationships by watching the parents interact with one another. Feelings of jealousy may develop between father and child. The father may find himself reacting to the child with impatience and resentment. The couple must be alert for imbalances of this nature in the family and come to terms with them before any harm is done to any member of the family.

The child should begin to feel secure in father's presence and affection. Although perhaps not present as often as the mother, the father's regular comings and goings give the child a sense of time. The child also discovers a new form of affection. The relationship is built on presence and an exchange of concern. The nature of affection received from the mother and father and the relationship that husband and wife share form the base from which the child will form all successive human relationships.

This enumeration of your responsibilities is not included to discourage or frighten you. It is to help you with your part in the child's life and to encourage you to face any difficulties, which seem very small in comparison with the immense joys you will discover in your fatherhood.

FOR GRANDPARENTS

As grandparents you have a tremendous interest in your grandchildren, which will affect the parents' and baby's lives in many ways. You (especially if you live close by) provide emotional and often practical support to the new family. You may help with tasks that the new parents are unfamiliar with, or relieve them of responsibilities when they become tired. Having an experienced, concerned adult around will make their day-to-day routine go more smoothly.

Your extra help will undoubtedly be welcome, but you may

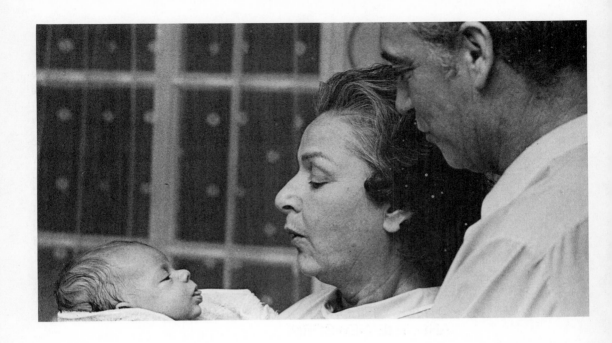

find that some aspects of your concern are considered annoying. This probably won't be a major difficulty, but you should try to keep the relationship as kindly as possible. Undoubtedly you will reminisce about raising your own children, and about how child-raising techniques have changed. This change in techniques may cause friction between grandparents and parents. Consider the simple aspects of clothing a baby. You may want to put a few sweaters on the baby, and your grandchild's parents would prefer to keep him or her lightly dressed. Consider these situations with tact, while understanding the concern that is being shown.

Remember that you are entering a new situation, even though you may not be aware of it. Now that your daughter or son has a child, you can no longer regard her or him as a child. You are probably becoming aware that your offspring are *really* adults now, and you must relinquish the last bit of parental protectiveness. Don't act as if you know much more about childcare than they do; don't be annoyed if they seem to doubt your judgment. They should try to accept your advice with affection, and remember that a short time ago they were your "little ones." For your own sake, everyone should try to keep family ties as amiable as possible.

TO MOTHERS

Before the child is born, explain to your parents and/or in-laws how you and your husband intend to manage the house and your new responsibilities. Discuss new child-rearing techniques. Explain that you are sure that the traditional methods were excellent, but that you would like to raise your child in the manner you see fit. Make it clear that you welcome advice but that you need to decide how suggestions will fit into the family routine. Also mention that you and your husband need to take responsibility for the baby to build your own confidence in your new roles. Try to avoid anything that will impede the smooth running of your household. If you need assistance, ask for it, but don't give the impression that you and your husband are not handling your situation.

OTHER CHILDREN AND THE NEWBORN

The arrival of a new baby poses problems for children. This fact has been known for a long time. Each family handles the situation differently. We would like to analyze the common reactions of other children, to help you avoid some of the pitfalls.

The Young Child (1 or 2 Years Old)

At this age, the child's world is still centered on you. The thought of being separated from you for a few days will make your child feel anxious and fearful. To alleviate some of this fear, you must make some advance preparations.

Late in your pregnancy (because children have a limited ability to comprehend and remember details) you should tell the child that soon he or she will have a little brother or sister. Start to set up the area of the house where the baby will be staying. Try to keep changes to a minimum, so that the older child won't feel displaced by the baby. Make arrangements for the care of the child during your absence. Psychologically, it is best for the child to stay at home where everything is familiar. He or she can be cared for by a grandparent and your husband.

It may not be practical to do this because of job demands. If this is the case, you may need to leave the child at his or her

grandparents' home while you are away. This is more practical, but it may cause more anxiety for the child. In addition to being suddenly deprived of mother and father, who provide security for day-to-day existence, the child must also adjust to a new routine and environment. This will be difficult, even though the child will be with loving people. To alleviate this distress, visit the house where the child will be staying several times before you go into the hospital. This will take some of the shock out of the situation and may even make the child look forward to the visit.

Your husband should visit the child often. Perhaps a gift will make the child feel better about the whole thing. If children are allowed to visit mothers at your hospital, take some time to play and talk with him or her.

When you arrive back home, your older child will probably be impatient to get back to the normal routine. At this time, you and your husband will be preoccupied with the baby. Your older child may feel rejected because you must spend so much time on the baby. Take special time for the older child. Play games, or give a small present to him or her. Make sure that you converse with him or her during the day. If you must reprimand the child, do so gently.

After having presented him or her with the new baby, don't expect the older child to accept this intruder immediately. Soon this reluctance may change to a curiosity that you may find interferes with your daily routine. Be patient, and don't get angry if the child gets in the way. Let him or her help you out with the multitudinous tasks you must do. This will give the older child a feeling of importance and belonging. It will also help him or her to get to know the new arrival.

Preschool Children

Many of the previous suggestions also apply to this age group. Additional precautions and explanations are also necessary, but they must be geared to the curiosity and more highly developed intelligence of children in this age group. Your absence followed by your return could be interpreted as abandonment and transfer of affection to the newborn. The amount of time that must be spent on the baby will probably accentuate any fears that the older child is experiencing. Even if your child is in a preschool program and is used to being separated from you for periods of time, you must still prepare him or her for the coming separation. This is true even if the child seems to be accepting the whole idea well.

When your child finds out that you are having a baby, he or she will undoubtedly have questions as to how the baby began. The questions deserve clear answers the child can understand. Fairy tales about storks or detailed discourses on embryology and gynecology are useless. Try to relate your answers to something your child is already aware of. Let the child feel the movements of the baby. This will make the understanding clearer. These discussions can be an excellent base for your child's sex education. The child will probably want to know the sex and name of the child and will use similar questions as a prelude for discussing the baby. The child wants to learn as much as possible about the new arrival. You should be aware that the child imagines that the baby will be as developed as he or she is, that an instant playmate will come home from the hospital. To avoid disappointment, show the child several babies, and explain that the new brother or sister will look like these small babies.

Hospital visits are often prohibited to small children. Maintain frequent contact by telephone, and tell him or her all about the new baby. Ask if he or she is having fun with daddy, and generally show an interest in the details of the child's life.

Reestablish contact with the child by talking alone while the baby is asleep. Play for a while, and talk about what happened during your absence. Then bring up the subject of the new baby. Paint a happy picture of playing together in a few years, and tell him or her how enjoyable the new addition will be. Discuss how much the new child will be able to learn from the older child, and how important he or she will be to the baby's growth. If these remarks are not well received, don't force them on the child.

Soon the older child will want to see the baby. Be prepared for varying reactions. Often the child will show a joyous curiosity in the new brother or sister. The child will probably examine the baby and remark on his or her features. He or she may want to touch and hold the baby. Let the child do this under your supervision, and don't give the impression that you are afraid for the baby when your older child is handling him or her.

The older child may not be so interested in the baby initially. Let the child come to the baby as he or she desires, and don't reprimand for his or her attitude. Ask the older child for small services in the day-to-day care of the baby, such as fetching a diaper or picking out an outfit for the baby to wear. Both you and your husband will probably want to show your older child extra affection during this time, and a special trip or gift may assure him or her of your love.

The numerous services that a newborn demands may seem to be unnecessary to your older child and may be a source of frustration and jealousy. Your older child may demand the same attentions from you. Telling him or her "You're too big for that" will probably be interpreted as a rejection. Try to attend to the needs of the baby without the presence of the other child, or ask for assistance if the child is present. If you don't understand what the older child really desires from you, he or she may regress to the behavior habits of a younger age. He or she may refuse to eat with a spoon or may suddenly become "un" toilet-trained.

Feeding can become the battleground where many of these feelings are worked out. If you are bottle feeding the baby, the older child may also demand a bottle. If you refuse this demand, the bottle may become a coveted item. Instead, give the child a bottle, but reward the child lavishly for drinking from a cup or glass. If you are breast feeding, the older child may also show an interest. He or she may ask many questions about the origin of the milk and may want to taste it. Permit the child to do this. Afterward, you will both agree that this milk is really only suitable for babies.

The School-age Child

The personality of the school-age child is more established than that of the preschooler. The child is also more independent of you. These two factors make the new arrival less of a threat than for a young child. Young boys may only show a superficial interest in the baby, but young boys are sensitive to their mother's feelings toward them. So you should not try to push the child into a stage of development that he's not prepared for. He is still a child, and you and your husband are still his parents.

Young girls identify a great deal with their mothers at this stage and may accept some part of the responsibility for the care of the child. They, too, however, are still young children and should not be pushed into accepting a role as "little mother."

Adolescents

Sexual questions preoccupy children of this age. Announcing a pregnancy produces diverse reactions and gives an indication of their progress in coming to terms with their own sexuality. The pregnancy makes evident to the adolescent a fact that they may not have considered or wanted to consider, mainly, that their parents share sexual relations. The relationship between the parents and the explanations that they have received about sex in the past determine the reactions of the adolescent. It is important to deal sensitively and straightforwardly with any issues that your adolescent brings up during this time.

If the family relations are good, the pregnancy will be met with joy and satisfaction. The adolescent may see it as an affirmation of his or her parent's youth. In other cases the adolescent may be embarrassed and may even have to work out some attitudes with the help of a psychiatrist or psychologist. Most often, the reactions are mixed and become more favorable as time goes on.

Reactions after the child is born vary from person to person. Boys often have no problems accepting the new baby. Adolescent girls, however, are in a more delicate stage of development. They are starting to mature sexually and are experimenting with this new element of their personality. They may see their pregnant mother as a denial of the desirability that they are trying to achieve, and not show an interest in the child. They may also be competing with the mother for the father's attention and may be contrasting their own physical appearance with that of their mother. Or they may reject their developing sexuality and completely submerge themselves into the maternal role. You should be aware of these two extreme reactions. They may explain erratic behavior on the part of your adolescent daughter. Try to remain open to her during this time.

THE SINGLE MOTHER

The number of single women who have children increases every year. Although having a child as a single woman is more widely accepted than in the past, many problems still exist for the single mother. Raising a child alone remains a difficult task for the woman involved.

Single women have children for many different reasons, and each situation differs. Some women are living with men without

being formally married. These women are not really single, except from a legal standpoint. Many women may not wish to marry the father of their child or may not be able to. In these cases the responsibility for the child's upbringing unfortunately rests solely on the mother. The main challenge is to provide stable circumstances for the child to grow up in. This is the concern of both the mother and certain social agencies. Programs are available to assist the single mother. Anyone in this situation should check with local agencies for assistance.

Now we would like to consider the psychological relationship between mother and child and to describe a few common pitfalls. Circumstances vary with each case, of course. The mother must make all the decisions herself. Relations with her own family and with the father of the child often disrupt the mother-child relationship.

The first step is to keep the family and any other relationships that the mother is involved in on as mature and supportive a base as possible. It is important that the child not be the only important relationship the mother has, that the child does not become the center of the mother's emotional life. To be sure, it is not easy to do this, but if it doesn't happen, the mother risks smothering the child with misplaced affection. The best thing the mother can give the child is a secure image of herself. It is important that the mother be happy and open to the outside world.

Sometimes the immensity of the role frightens single mothers, and they become confused as to how to be mother and father to this child. In this confusion, they may come to resent the child, and the result may be hurt feelings between mother and child. The mother should try to provide the best financial support she can but remember that the shaping and development of the child's personality is more important than simply meeting physical needs.

Some single mothers bear a grudge against the child. They may think that the child resulted from a mistake, that it is unfair to have to be responsible for the child's upbringing. They may feel guilty about the child's existence. These feelings of guilt may be reinforced by the family of the mother. It is important for the single mother to be aware of how the opinions of others may affect her and to maintain a clear mind as to who is of real assistance to her and who is complicating her life. It is important for her to protect her child from guilt that may be conferred on him or her as a result of the circumstances of birth. This is not easy to do, and she may need additional help from a social worker or psychologist to sort out the circumstances of her life and to deal with them.

Sometimes a mother may unconsciously use her child to work out her own problems. Sometimes the child is used as a means to sever a difficult or abusive relationship with her own parents. At other times, having a child as a single woman may be a way of resolving a difficult relationship with her father. Sometimes a mother projects her own uncertainties on the child. These situations can be disastrous for the environment in which the child will grow up. Any problems of this nature must be dealt with honestly and courageously for the sake of the child and the mother.

We are not describing these situations to make an already difficult situation worse. We only want to point them out so that the single mother is aware of them and will be able to recognize them if they develop. Many single mothers raise children well and have excellent relationships with them. The untraditional nature of the family does not mean that the family cannot be full of joy and happiness. However, even if the parent-child relationship is good, the mother should try to have her child develop relationships with men she trusts. The fact that the man is not the real father is not all-important. The child should see a stability and sureness in the man and be aware that his or her mother trusts him.

All of these things will not happen without effort, and the mother must be aware that enormous sacrifices will have to be made. However, the rewards of bringing up a well-rounded, happy child will compensate for the sacrifices.

11

CONTAGIOUS DISEASES

From the time of birth on, you will probably have many visitors. You will probably notice that some of these people are not completely healthy, and you may begin to worry about the germs the baby is being exposed to. For this reason, we are including a section on the effects various illnesses have on newborns.

The most dangerous of these infections originate from microbes of the staphylococcus family. This type of germ may be found in several varied diseases (which may occur with other problems)—for example, throat, mouth, or nasal infections or common digestive and respiratory troubles.

Throat infections come from many sources. Some, like diphtheria, are quite rare today. However, sore throats (tonsillitis, pharyngitis) are frequently caused by streptococcus and staphylococcus, and such infections are very dangerous for your baby.

Rhinitis and other "colds" are inflammations of the nasal mucous membranes. They afflict the nasal passages and higher portions of the throat and usually begin as viral infections (the common cold is a good example). Microbial germs can reinfect the susceptible areas and may be transmitted to your baby. Germs of this nature are generally spread by coughing.

Several types of respiratory infections are contagious (bronchitis, pneumonia, pleurisy) but do not pass unnoticed, and it should never occur to anyone afflicted by one of these diseases to visit your baby.

Digestive problems, particularly diarrhea, can result from

Health Problems That Affect the Newborn

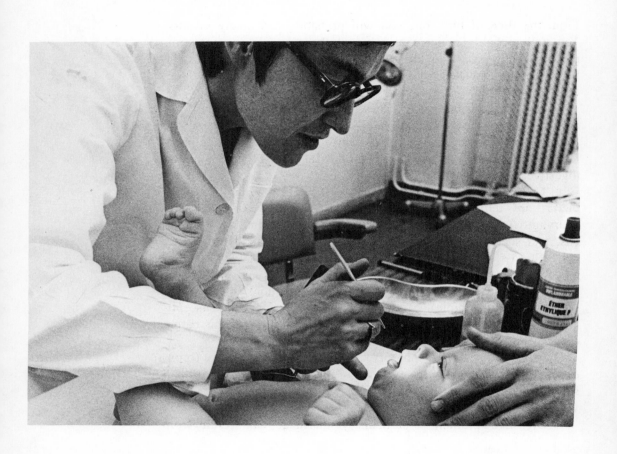

many things. Sometimes it is a microbial cause, and the most dangerous are the latent infections (by staphylococcus or *E. coli,* for instance). Such germs are transmitted to your baby when nipples, bottles, or the like are handled directly by a person who is infected.

Dental abscess is a very common disease and may be thought of as a nest of various germs, principally staphylococcus, too.

Skin infections can be of various types, including impetigo and paronychia, which is an inflammation of the skinfold around the fingernail and is dangerous because it is staphylococcic in origin. Other skin problems, such as eczema, can be sites for further infection. These afflictions are spread through direct contact or through objects that have touched an infected person.

Eye infections, such as conjunctivitis, blepharitis (inflammation of the edges of the eyelid), and chalazion (a small, hard tumor that develops on the eyelid) are transmitted in the same way as are skin infections.

Although tuberculosis is no longer common, it is so serious to the newborn that we want to mention it. Anyone with this disease should not be near a newborn baby for any reason. Anyone with a cough (even if it appears to stem from other causes, such as excess smoking or a bronchial infection) should not be around the baby. If the person has undetected TB (which is not impossible, since many people have not had chest X-rays to find out if they have it), the germs will be spread through coughing. People having regular contact with the baby should consider having a chest X-ray to rule out TB. This is not a difficult problem if it is included with regular physical examinations.

Through elementary hygiene and precautions, most diseases can be avoided. It is possible for an intermediate person to transmit the disease, but certain conditions must take place for this to happen. Most important, the intermediary must have been in contact both with the sick person and with the baby over a short interval of time. Hygienic precautions will probably prevent infection even in these circumstances.

Illnesses that are not caused by germs pose no danger of being transmitted to newborn infants. Examples include asthma, allergic rhinitis, and allergic tracheitis (inflammation of the trachea). These afflictions have symptoms similar to infections resulting from germs, but because they stem from an allergic reaction, they are not contagious.

If you have had measles, chicken pox, German measles, or mumps, your baby is *theoretically* immune to them for the first month. This immunity occurs because your antibodies are still present in his or her system. Nonetheless, it is preferable that the child not come in contact with any diseases in this category. If you have not had one of these diseases, and your child has been exposed to it, you must contact your doctor *immediately*, for proper measures to be taken.

Thrush is a yeast infection of the mouth and throat that affects young children. It is characterized by white patches and ulcers, and eventually inflammation of the intestinal tract. Adults often transmit the disease. It is found in the mouth, on skin, and in the vagina. Use of antibiotics favors a latent proliferation of this microorganism.

The newborn can become contaminated during childbirth if the mother's genital tract contains the fungus. Or the fungus can be on an object that touches the child's lips. The mouth is the type of environment in which the fungus grows well. An infant's saliva does not perform as a cleansing agent, as does an adult's. For this reason, milk residue and acidification of the mouth favor the growth of the fungus.

During the first stage, the mouth dries out, and the tongue takes on a reddish color. The tongue loses its natural covering, and the taste buds rise in relief from the surface of the tongue. The interior of the cheeks also dries out. The mucous membrane, which is normally pink, becomes more reddish in color. It also appears to be less shiny.

During the second stage, white spots form on the tongue, the roof of the mouth, and sometimes on the interior of the cheeks. Eating becomes difficult. The baby nurses feebly or leaves a lot of milk in the bottle. Often a rash resulting from the same fungus appears around the baby's anus.

Simple hygienic measures will prevent the child from contracting this disease. Washing your hands before handling the baby's bottles or nipples and sterilization of feeding items will destroy any fungus that the baby would come in contact with. If the baby still gets thrush, many doctors recommend washing out the baby's mouth with a solution of bicarbonate water. Put 1 teaspoon in a glass of water. Several washings a day may be necessary to control the problem. You should also contact your doctor if you notice any signs of thrush.

SKIN PROBLEMS

Several common skin problems can trouble a newborn. Generally, these can be cleaned up through good hygienic measures. Although other skin problems can afflict babies, we will not discuss them because they are quite rare and require the attention of a specialist.

Skin Problems of the Head and Face

Whiteheads and other acnelike formations may develop on the face and head of an infant. Although more common in the past, it is still seen today with some frequency. Today we understand the causes of it and are able to treat it more successfully.

During the days following childbirth, hormonal imbalances develop in the child's system. These imbalances are caused by the abrupt withdrawal of placental hormones and the lack of steady hormone production by the child. This causes the oil glands to secrete more oil than is necessary. The causes of infant skin disruptions are very similar to the causes of adolescent skin problems.

The face of the baby may develop signs that resemble acne. The cheeks and nasal area may be particularly affected. If the mother has a yeast infection in her birth canal, these organisms can also start infections in the affected areas. A thorough cleansing of the baby during the first 2 days will prevent this.

Brownish or yellowish patches may appear on the scalp. These can be removed gently, without difficulty. They are found most often on the crown and anterior section of the scalp. In some cases, the forehead and eyebrows may be affected. Washing the scalp every 2 or 3 days will prevent their appearance.

Miliaria is more a characteristic of the skin than the condition described above. It appears most often during the days following birth. On the forehead, around the nose, and on the chin you may notice small pinhead-sized dots of white. They are deposits of excess oil which sometimes become infected. When this happens, a small red area surrounds the oil deposit. This condition is referred to as miliaria acne. Treatment is very simple. Don't put any oily products on the child's face (such as bath or baby oils) and avoid using harsh soaps, as they will increase oil production. Simply wash the baby's face daily with water. Tap water will suffice. If you feel that your town's water supply contains too many impurities, you can use a mild bottled water.

Diaper Rash and Similar Problems

Erythema is a general term for any diffused redness of the skin. Causes are varied. To be sure, wet diapers and resulting ammonia fermentation are a major cause of rashes on the buttocks. Irritating substances, such as detergents or fabric softeners, can cause rashes. Perfumed products are also irritating to tender skin. Occasionally synthetic fabrics cause a reaction. Infections from intestinal germs (streptococci, staphylococci) can be embedded in the folds of the baby's skin. Yeast infections from the digestive tract also will cause redness on the buttocks.

Often it is possible to find out what is causing a rash by noting the area of the buttocks that is affected. If the redness surrounds the anus, a yeast infection is often responsible. If the redness is in the folds of the baby's skin, bacteria from the feces may well be the culprit. Irritation of the pubic area may also be from a bacterial source. If the irritation is on the crown of the buttocks, wet diapers are probably causing the problem.

Frequent changes, washing of the genital and anal area with mild soap, and use of cotton diapers washed with a gentle detergent (and without any rinse products) will clear up the majority of these problems. Your doctor may prescribe an antiseptic or antimycotic, if a fungus infection is responsible for the rash.

Irritations in the Folds of the Baby's Skin

These irritations can appear in any of the folds on the baby's body. A red, irregular line that follows the contour of the fold marks this type of irritation. The moistness in these folds favors bacterial and fungal growth. Careful washing will prevent these problems from developing in most cases. If they appear anyway, washing with a mild antiseptic soap daily will eliminate them. Your doctor will be able to advise you on this situation.

Other Skin Problems

Impetigo is a skin infection resulting from streptococci and staphylococci germs. It is contagious and develops from contact with a person having it. Reddish sores are found on all parts of the body. They are 1/8 to 1/4 inch in diameter and are filled with a clear liquid that becomes yellow as time passes. The bubble breaks, leaving behind a reddish sore. General health is not affected, but treatment is necessary to avoid spreading the disease.

The treatment most often prescribed is applying warm compresses soaked in a potassium permanganate solution and soaking of the crusts with soapy water. To avoid infection yourself, wash your hands with soap before and after handling the baby. Wash the baby with a mildly antiseptic soap. Boil and iron any garments that have come in direct contact with the baby's skin.

Sometimes small, raised red dots appear on a baby's skin. Often this type of eruption appears on the cheeks and around the mouth. The skin may also be flaky and crusty. This condition may be mistaken for eczema, but it is usually the result of some sort of irritation. The infant may be burping up milk while sleeping. The milk dries around the child's mouth and irritates the skin. A perfumed product (soap, bath oil, or cologne) may be the cause. Detergents that are too strong or rinse products can also cause a reaction. Eczema is very rare among newborn infants.

DIGESTIVE PROBLEMS

Regurgitation and Vomiting

The difference between vomiting and regurgitation lies in the use of the stomach and abdominal muscles. More force is used in vomiting. It is also accompanied by a feeling of nausea and sickness. Mainly it is the muscles of the stomach that are used in regurgitation, and a feeling of nausea is not present. It is sometimes difficult to tell the difference between the two in newborns.

Regurgitation is usually not traumatic and happens after feedings. The child may burp up a teaspoon or so of milk. Sometimes the quantity that is burped up is so small that it doesn't even come out of the child's mouth. This is normal and is no cause for alarm.

Volume and significance of vomiting vary from case to case. The baby may vomit up milk from time to time for no apparent reason. The milk will have a different appearance depending on how long the milk has been in the stomach (normal if it was just eaten, and curdled if some time has passed since the feeding). Sometimes a clear liquid is passed up, which is simply a coagulation of milk in the stomach. The causes of vomiting can be varied. A simple infection, such as a nasal inflammation, can cause it. Or it may be a symptom of a more serious problem, such as a lung infection, meningitis, or intestinal virus. Problems needing surgical intervention (hernia or peritonitis) can also cause vomiting. If this is the case, fever, a refusal to eat, and a disruption of normal activity patterns are also present. Continued crying also accompanies this type of problem.

If the baby is vomiting up large quantities of milk, it may be that the formula is not suited to the child's digestive system. An insufficient amount can also cause vomiting.

Congenital abnormalities such as pyloric stenosis (a constricting of the lower end of the stomach) are a frequent cause of repeated vomiting. With this particular disorder, vomiting usually starts during the second or third week. Soon after each feeding, the child will vomit up large quantities of milk. Various common solutions do not work, and the child may begin to lose weight. An X-ray will reveal the problem, and a simple surgical procedure may be necessary to correct it. Some babies have an abnormality of the joining of the stomach and the esophagus. A hiatal hernia (upward protrusion of the stomach into the esophagus) or an incontinent cardia (orifice that joins the stomach and the esophagus) can cause some vomiting after feedings. Simple treatments with anti-spasmodics can relieve the problem. Thickening of the milk with mucilages also brings vomiting under control until the child can digest solid foods. Sometimes no cause can be found for repeated vomiting. Doctors may conclude that the digestive system cannot handle an all-liquid diet. In these cases, general health is good, and the baby retains his or her appetite. Treatment with antispasmodics and milk thickeners may be helpful. The problem usually clears up in a few months.

In general, regurgitation is a physiologic function and no cause for alarm. Vomiting can be a symptom of something more serious, but most often is not. If you see that your child vomits with regularity, you should call your doctor so that the cause of the problem can be determined.

If the problem is repeated, you can give the child sugar water until you hear from the doctor. Mix a teaspoon of sugar with 4 ounces of water, and give it to the baby at the rate of about ½ ounce every hour.

Diarrhea

As is the case with vomiting, diarrhea can be caused by many factors. Infection and an unsatisfactory feeding program are the most common culprits.

Infectious diarrhea results from the presence of germs in the intestine. Infection can stem from contamination of formula or bottles. It can also come from a lack of personal hygiene of people caring for the child. If the infection is nasal in origin, it is practically impossible to avoid spreading it to the baby, because germs are transmitted in speaking and breathing. Many varieties of germs can cause diarrhea, and analysis of the feces is the only way to determine which one is causing the problem. One test used to diagnose the type of germ present is Gram's stain. The material to be tested is stained. If dye is retained, the germ is Gram positive. Germs that don't take the dye include the normal bacteria of the intestine and colon. If no dye is retained, the germ is Gram negative.

The course that diarrhea takes depends on the germ causing it. Babies may have diarrhea and still maintain normal growth. Extremely liquid forms being passed 10 or 12 times a day with fever and refusal to eat or vomiting are cause for alarm. Dehydration will follow quickly with this type of situation. If any of these conditions occur, you must get in touch with your physician immediately.

Treatment can take on two aspects. The first is a dietetic approach. Binders are added to the diet to normalize the digestive system. Milk feeding may be interrupted depending on the seriousness of the situation. The second type of treatment is of a medical variety. The goal is to eliminate the germ causing the diarrhea. Antibiotics or antiseptics are administered.

Sometimes diarrhea is caused from outside the digestive system. Other symptoms (loss of weight, refusing to eat) may or may not accompany it. Fecal examinations are negative in this situation. A complete physical examination is necessary to determine the cause.

Intolerance to diet is a less common cause of diarrhea, although it is usually the first area that the mother suspects. In fact, intolerance to milk is quite rare, and many tests are required to verify its existence. If it is the problem, it shows itself after a few weeks of life. Vegetable substitutes for milk are given to the child, and normal growth continues. Often the child is intolerant to one element in the milk.

One type of diarrhea, called postprandial diarrhea, is particular to breast feeding. It is characterized by a movement during or immediately following the feeding. The movements are quite liquid, containing lumps, and are often greenish. The problem shows up early, usually during the second week. Appetite is not affected, and the child continues to gain weight. Diaper rash and some vomiting and regurgitation often accompany this form of diarrhea. This often happens to high-strung infants. They may wake up at the slightest noise and do not sleep through the night easily. Infection plays no part in the problem. Vigorous and rapid contractions in the large intestine cause insufficiently digested, unassimilated sugars to ferment. A lactic acid is produced that irritates the digestive tract. This problem does not occur with formula, because cow's milk contains elements that neutralize the lactic acid.

The quality of mother's milk is not the cause of the problem, and switching to bottle feeding is not warranted in this situation. The difficulty can be treated with buffer-based products that neutralize the acid in question.

Colic

Colic often begins after the child has been fed. It may occur every day at a given time. Most often, it takes place regularly every night at about 6 P.M. The baby cries, waves his or her arms and legs, and generally acts as if gas is causing the difficulty. Then he or she burps, calms down for a few moments, and begins crying again. This can go on for an hour or two. It is not the result of not getting enough to eat or from a digestive infection. The baby gains weight, and general health is good. The colic begins between the tenth and fifteenth day, and often ends at the end of the third month. Many causes are suspected, including formula incompatibility, allergies, an immature digestive system, or early psychosomatic disease. Examinations reveal nothing serious. As physical causes are eliminated, other facts become more noticeable. This sort of colic often occurs in babies who are nervous and who react to the smallest amount of attention. Often the mother is an anxious person, and a feverish atmosphere pervades the home. This type of colic often disappears when the child is placed in the care of another person or when the environment is modified.

At night the child's mother is exhausted from her daily activities. A meal may well be scheduled for this time, making life more difficult. If her husband is immature and/or reluctant to fulfill his share of the responsibility for his child, she is probably apprehensive about his presence, as well. As a result, she is tense, and the climate of the home reflects this.

Treating this type of situation is difficult. It is not easy to tell the mother to change her reactions to situations when that has been her pattern. It is more difficult still to try to demand mature and responsible behavior from a new father who may simply not be willing to try to grow up. In this case, the mother should try to ignore any obligations beyond achieving a calm household. Treating the infant begins with making him or her feel more secure in the home. Calm the baby by holding him or her in your arms, rocking the baby while holding him or her lying close to your body on his or her stomach, and eventually giving the child a pacifier. Denying a pacifier (especially if it helps the situation) on philosophical grounds in this case is ridiculous. It may be helpful to give the baby his or her daily bath at the time when colic is most common.

Refusing to Eat

At one time or another your baby may refuse to eat, or may sleep through a feeding. This is not serious, and you should not become alarmed. The next feeding will come sooner than usual, and the baby will eat vigorously. The disruption in the schedule will be made up the next day.

On the other hand, if the baby skips feedings regularly, or is leaving significant quantities of milk in the bottle or breast, you should alert your doctor. Refusing to eat can be the first symptom of illness.

Take the baby's temperature, and make a note of how much milk the baby has been taking. Relate your findings to your doctor. Sometimes the reason is simple. Perhaps the mother ate something (such as asparagus) that made her milk unappetizing. Perhaps the baby doesn't like the taste of the formula. Some like their milk more acidic or more sugared. Some won't drink their milk unless it is more sugared. In these cases, an adjustment to suit the baby is all that is necessary, but it is also necessary to mention that these situations are not very frequent.

In other cases, a minor infection may be present. Nasal infections, diarrhea, or gastrointestinal upsets are common. In small infants, ear infections can develop without fever or pain. In some cases, examination of blood, urine, and chest X-rays may be necessary to discover the problem.

Constipation

Constipation mainly affects babies who are being raised on formula, although it exists in breast-fed babies and is usually tied to the mother's problems with constipation. Infant constipation requires treatment with common medications.

For infants who are on formula, changing to a special mother-like milk will solve the difficulty. This is a better solution than adding laxatives or oil to the milk. Breast-fed babies will benefit by mixing 2 or 3 ounces of water with an equal amount of orange juice and adding it to their diet. Your doctor may also advise that you give a small amount of cereal to the baby. He or she may also recommend that you drink more fluids to improve your own system.

Use of glycerin suppositories might be considered in episodic cases. Regular use of these devices can lead to a dependence on them, however. In most cases, additional fluids or a low-sugar formula will solve the problem.

Occlusion

Intestinal occlusion, which is an abnormal closure of the intestine, is very rare in infants. A halting of the digestive processes results from this. Occlusions can happen for a variety of reasons.

The absence of primary feces (meconium) and frequent vomiting of bile and milk quickly indicate that a problem exists, and tests to determine its nature are begun immediately.

Reasons for the problem vary. The esophagus may be malformed, or a prenatal membrane between the anus and the rectum may not have been reabsorbed. This is called an imperforate anus. Obstructions can occur along the intestines, or secretions that aid passage of the meconium may not be present (ileus meconial).

These situations are very rare and necessitate surgical intervention in the hospital. In premature infants occlusions are often the result of intestinal contractions and not of any obstruction of the system. Simple medications clear up the difficulty in these circumstances.

RESPIRATORY DIFFICULTIES

Infants who are several months old are subject to a variety of minor respiratory difficulties. Newborns, on the other hand, are seldom affected by any type of respiratory problem. When a difficulty of this nature befalls them, however, it is usually of a serious nature.

Infants who are a few months old have been exposed to a variety of temperatures, people, and germs. They must depend on their own defenses. The newborn lives in a relatively secure world. Few people handle him or her, and the baby is still protected by the mother's immunities. Bronchial pneumonia, pneumonia, and bronchitis are very rare during the first month. Allergies also do not become apparent during this time. All of these difficulties are more common in older infants.

This is not to say that there are no respiratory problems in newborns. They are usually accompanied by a general decline in health (refusal to eat, lack of weight gain or even weight loss, vomiting and diarrhea). Signs of respiratory distress (irregular breathing, fighting suffocation) are also present. There is a greater chance of respiratory problems in premature infants of low birth weight, in babies who have been through long and difficult labors, and in those who may have contracted infections from their mothers.

Some children have a minor congenital breathing problem called congenital stridor. Respiration is quite noisy. You may not notice it immediately. After a few weeks you may hear a soft rattle when the baby breathes in. The amount of noise varies and may even disappear, depending on the position of the child's head. It may be more marked during feedings. Other than this minor difficulty, the child eats normally and gains weight. There is no nasal discharge. The sound does not result from a disease but from a softness in the throat which vibrates when the baby breathes in. This most often affects boys and disappears in a few months to a year. No treatment is known. It is only necessary that you keep an eye on the child to make sure that no infections develop.

CONVULSIONS

Any convulsion that occurs soon after birth is usually a sign of serious disturbance. A convulsion is recognizable by a brief trembling (several seconds long) that affects one or several extremities and sometimes the face. It is often difficult to determine if a convulsion has actually occurred, because trembling can take place for a number of reasons that have nothing to do with brain functions. Sometimes the convulsion affects only the muscles of the trunk. The muscles contract, and trembling may happen at the same time.

Causes of convulsions are serious and varied. The most frequent include fever, cerebral hemorrhage, meningitis, metabolic disturbances, and illnesses contracted during the fetal stage (German measles, toxoplasmosis).

If you think that your child may have had a convulsion, you *must* contact your doctor *immediately*. If your baby eats well, is growing, sleeps well, and was born in a normal labor, chances are that you are mistaken. Nonetheless, an examination of the child should be performed by the doctor. He or she will check the baby over and probably tell you that the baby was only experiencing a trembling movement, that no convulsion has taken place. You should feel no embarrassment or hesitancy in contacting your doctor in a situation like this.

If your baby was born after a difficult labor, cries or sleeps for a very long period of time, eats poorly, does not put on weight, or has a fever, call your doctor *immediately*, and take the baby to the nearest hospital. If you think that you notice a convulsion in conjunction with fever, quick action is imperative.

HEAT STROKE

Heat stroke occurs in summer, but also occurs during the winter months when the baby stays in a poorly ventilated, overheated room, or lies in direct sunlight. The baby is probably overdressed for the temperature of the room. If the thermostat shows a temperature of around 85°, the room is overheated. The baby will show signs of discomfort, refuse to eat, and cry inconsolably.

Take the baby's temperature with a rectal thermometer that has been well lubricated with petroleum jelly. If the temperature is around 99° or 100° F, heat stroke may be the reason for the child's discomfort. Call your doctor to rule out other reasons for an elevated temperature. While waiting for the doctor to call back, redress the baby in lighter clothing, and either ventilate the room or move him or her to a cooler room. Give the baby some water that is room temperature. If more serious signs of heat stroke develop, such as vomiting, diarrhea, or torpor (abnormal inactivity), take the baby to the nearest hospital immediately.

CONGENITAL HEART PROBLEMS

These are abnormalities that affect the valves between the atria and ventricles or the walls that separate the right and left portions of the heart, and sometimes the main blood vessel leading away from the heart. These abnormalities can cause a variety of circulatory problems, some very minor, some quite serious. Some affect the ability to live; others are not found except by careful examination.

Cyanosis is a bluish color of the skin resulting from poor circulation. It may be permanent, or show up only when the child is putting forth effort, during a feeding, for example.

Various respiratory difficulties can result from congenital heart problems. These can include difficult respiration, or chronic bronchitis.

Examinations during the first days of life usually uncover significant heart defects, although abnormalities may pass unnoticed during these early days or weeks. If growth seems abnormally slow, further examination may show this to be the cause.

CONGENITAL DISLOCATION OF THE HIP

This problem is not obvious at birth until the doctor performs a simple test for it that is routinely included in postnatal examinations. If the dislocation is discovered, it can be treated easily. If it is not discovered, the child will have difficulty learning to walk and will walk with a limp.

Basically, congenital dislocation of the hip is a flattening of the normally round hip socket. The head of the femur bone fits into the hip at this point. If the socket is not shaped properly, the leg does not join the hip correctly. If discovered at birth, it can be corrected by keeping the thighs apart, thereby forcing the head of the femur into the socket. By doing this, the socket grows into a normal shape. Special cushions are designed for this purpose. The joint will be normal by the time the child begins to walk. Usually the problem clears up through correct treatment before 1 year of age.

This problem affects girls (80 to 90% of cases) more than boys, and more often affects the left hip than the right. As it is hereditary, certain families show a predisposition to it, but its causation is also related to environment. Congenital hip dislocation occurs more frequently in babies who are breech births.

Examination for it is routine and consists of the following test. The baby is laid on his or her back with knees and hips bent and thighs pulled out toward the sides of the body. As the thigh is pulled outward, a "click" can be felt as the head of the femur slides into the hip socket. When the thigh is moved back in, toward the middle of the body, the click is again noticeable, as the ball of the femur slides out of the socket. The click is called "Ortolani's sign." X-rays will confirm the exact nature of the problem and determine the best method of treatment.

Index